Marianne E. Meyer

on Wheels

From Michelstadt
To Marrakech

The information introduced in this book was carefully researched and imparted in all conscience. However author and publisher don't take any liability for damages of any nature that could emerge directly or indirectly from the usage or application of the data in this book. The information is intended for interested parties and to share.

© 2014 by Marianne E. Meyer, Tavira, Portugal
All rights are with the author

drmarianneemeyer @ gmail.com
www.marianne-e-meyer.com

Cover design, record & layout: M. Meyer
Photo credits
Titel-page: Reinhard Lüth
Cover back: The Morocco Globetrotter
Inner part photos: Page 3 F. Nos; p.15,19,24,26, 39,47,55,58,61,67,71,74,85,87,89 M. Meyer; p. 88 Klaas Evenhuis, p. 85,88,89 C.-P. Meyer

Production and Publishing:
BoD - Books on Demand, Norderstedt
ISBN 978-3-7386-0957-8

Some more books by M. E. Meyer:

Thus, water connects our worlds
Doris Day and My Search for Relatives
Spirulina, Survival Food for a New Age
Psyllium - So bekommen Sie Ihr Fett weg
Cranberry Power Frucht
Wunderwesen Wasser: Clusterwasser stoppt Allergie, Alzheimer, Krebs...
Spirulina, das blaugrüne Wunder

Marianne Meyer, Apardado 320
P-8801 Tavira

M. Meyer has traveled four continents. For her, it is always more important to understand the country and the people than to collect attractions.

Professionally, she has passed through many stages of life with the focus on self-help and learning: We are our own best teachers, healers, and spiritual leaders.

Formerly a Doctor's assistant, she later studied at *FHS* and *Johann-W.-Goethe University* in Frankfurt, laying emphasis on family therapy and gerontology, followed by a PhD study in gerontology and a study in nutrition, focusing on immune defense and Spirulina. After earning her PhD in nutrition and living more than ten years in the US, the author went back to the Frankfurt/Heidelberg area and introduced Spirulina to her European and Russian readers. Ms. Meyer currently lives in Portugal and works at times with juveniles, who are displaying behavioral problems.

TABLE OF CONTENTS ... 5

Introduction ... 6
D*ry*, stuffy air of central heating, goodbye ... 6
Visiting Bursins: Sandy & Sir Peter Ustinov ... 9
Sour is not funny ... 11
Hookers and the karmic law ... 13
Gibraltar, small country and *small-world phenomenon* ... 17
Ferry ride and entry ... 19
Déjà vu in Marrakesh ... 22
Second home *Banana Village* ... 29
Social contacts, helpers and social reforms ... 35
As chaff in the wind - daily routine on *The Plate* ... 38
Fetes, sand storms and other challenges ... 52
Approach to the past ... 59
Sexology & wishes under the moon atrial ... 63
Kafkaesque in Marrakesh ... 70
Water traps at Ouzoud waterfall ... 75
Two royal cities and a stormy ferry crossing ... 77
Sleepless in La Linea ... 79
New acquisition for the coincidence album ... 80
Saddish journey home ... 81
Postscript for the not quite confident ... 82
Acknowledgments ... 83

Choice of pitches ~ Camper peculiarities ... 84
Tips for the start of the tour ... 84
Addresses ... 84
Literature ... 85
Favorite recipes on tour ... 86
Plans for a wellness tour on wheels ... 88
For your notes ... 90

Foreword

Dear relatives, friends and interested parties, with this travel account I want to show you how Peter and I tend to outwit the winter. Also, I want to get to the bottom of my family's secret. It has already caused me to write two books, in the hope that one would fall into the right hands. Don't you think it is mega strange that not only the prominent relative of my mother lives in Carmel, but also the grandfather of my father is said to have settled there? Famous or unknown, I do not care. However, I am flirting with the idea of Henry Miller being related to my ancestor since his father was a tailor from Bavaria and his mother grew up in Hesse. Michelstadt is in Shanks' pony distance from the three-country triangle Baden-Württemberg, Bavaria and Hesse. Grandmother Maria's published poems and my father's writing ambitions speak for it. Henry Miller lived for ten years in the vicinity of Carmel. Although soaring in higher regions, he continually catches my attention. My friend Celeste was half a year his companion, and she told me some secrets. Somewhere I read Sagittariuses could not keep to themselves. I can! Too bad for you.

The way Henry presented himself in *Big Sur and the Oranges of Hieronymus Bosch*, he reminded me strongly of my brother Heinrich, who was also born on December 26. Could so many coincidences happen by chance? In our first apartment in California, my great-grandfather appeared to me as a ghost. I only know this much about him: The most likely New Apostolic emigrated from the Rhine-Main area to America after fathering the child of love on Christmas 1901. Searching for honor, Wilhelmina Meckes married in a hurry, and on October 5, 1902 Maria saw the light of day as a *7-month child*.

My great-grandfather took on the name Dieter Victor and used to live in the Carmel area.

Many, whom I informed about my ghost experience, believe in a dream. It does not matter since I saw my lean ancester with beetle brows and burn sides in a light blue shirt with rolled up sleeves and dark gray trousers. Could I leaf through the albums of all Northern California Victors, I would probably recognize him. Certainly, I was not 100% sure any longer, if I had understood the name correctly. German children are seldom brought up that they feel very sure about anything. However, since two months later, my mother told me this family secret of all things on a stroll through Carmel (!), I took that as confirmation. After all, all my maternal relatives have the so-called second sight. So, for Doris's 90th birthday, I wrote an autobiographical novel DORIS DAY AND MY SEARCH FOR RELATIVES. An oversized promotional postcard, explaining this *Carmel Family Mystery*, I sent to 15 Californian Victors. So far, a single feedback of a Mr. Victor from Odessa, via Facebook.

Dry, stuffy air of central heating, goodbye

The icy season had spread out its morbid cape, and crisp freeze had already eaten its way through all cracks. Our trend indicator fell every hour, especially that of Peter. We used to trim Father Frost's wings and eloped to the Canaries until we settled in the Pacific Ocean's most beautiful state. Which the Americans had been able to reap in the Mexican War in 1848. Currently, California is threatened by the Fukushima fallout. The karma strikes back!

We enjoyed living in the sunny paradise for ten years. Seven fat years we lived in our domicile, embedded in the Santa Monica Mountains, along with deer, raccoons, owls coyotes, and wild geese. However, because of the continual flow of guests from abroad, we hardly ever traveled. My pent-up demand for freedom and change was immense, especially after Thanksgiving with Celeste. The Ex-MGM-manager lived in Topanga, the hippie town west of L.A. There, we met Pia. The Swede had formerly modeled in Munich. We also talked of her famous colleague Uschi Obermaier. Pia raved about Uschi's luxury bus, with which the mother of all supermodels and her life mate Dieter Bockhorn traveled through Asia, USA and Mexico. I was on fire when Pia established the contact to the Bavarian.

The interview with Uschi caused me to have butterflies in the stomach and awakened my desire to travel. For me as a Saggy with Gemini Ascendant, this requires not much. I longed for diversification. I would have liked to have replaced our house with Uschi's bus for a year. My half-jokingly uttered offer she ignored and reported on her planned photo book through which she then managed a kind of comeback and was able to afford a house in Topanga. About their travels, I was not able to get out much from her. On the last common tour, her partner had bled to death in a motorcycle accident. We globetrotter must all reckon with losing our partners at the other end of the world. Luckily it does not discourage us.

Why we again landed in the German bad weather, I have explained in the Doris Day book extensively. So many things happened at once. Afterward, we were annoyed that we did not go to Bacha California or Belize, where life was much cheaper. However, the gaffe could not permanently ruin our mood because we did it like the migrant birds. We let ourselves grow wings in the form of an apartment on wheels. Since Peter was afraid it might not be our thing, we practiced first with an antiquated caravan of the exclusive brand Concorde. However, we got to a model with which even the manufacturer did not want to identify. Had it been up to me, we would have gotten a new camper at once. Gypsy blood may be running through my veins. After all, my grandfather was boatmen and constantly on the go on Neckar, Rhine and Waal to Rotterdam. Luckily we switched to a 1½ year old motor home.

When, on early January 2002 in Algeciras, we dashed with our Hymer as the last vehicle onto the ferry, we were hailed by Erika from Varel. She thought it was super cool as we got the tickets within half an hour, were buying the food for the journey and at the last minute reached the ship. She told some colleagues about it. Some time later the report on *Radio Camping* came back to us changed dramatically: the men had lowered down the ramp again when they saw us roaring through the harbor with 75 miles per hour ...

Our first tour, we took 1998/99 and lasted six months in Spain, Portugal and Morocco. Then we went only three months, since Peter like me turned his hobby into a profession. However, he was not able to work everywhere. It happened like this: When the stock market crashed in 2000, we lost almost all of our assets again. This happened to us three times by the way. I'd like to see anyone else do that! Being a millionaire three times, each time losing almost everything and start all again. In my astrological chart, it says that I'd have to learn to experience losses. Since I was raised to economy, I always got to partners who helped me to learn about losing. Edi hit my car, and Günther persuaded me to vouch for Edi's sister. Although, Peter had made me retract the money over the court, but with him I learned to let go big time.

My quest for safe investments answered my

soldier of fortune with a weary smile. However, this time, the whining was exceptionally heavy: What am I going to do? At my age, I can only be a garbage man. I pattered the encouraging saying I had often heard in California: *Do what you love to do, and the money will follow.* Alternatively, live your talents, and you are rich and happy. For me, this motto fell on fertile ground. My American friends say: We must act as if we have what we want already. Since reading and writing have always been my hobbies, I introduced myself as a writer and began writing travel reports about California, especially about how you can have fun without money. If you would like to explore the United States by car or RV, try my favorites:

1. On working days, we can enjoy a catchy tune in a box at the Hollywood Bowl. The musicians rehearse almost every day for a weekend concert and are much more relaxed than at their performances. Many members of the audience enjoy their picnic in the morning sun.

2. Lovers of rare art treasures can pass the time in the Paul Getty Museum. In 1976, the oil billionaire bequeathed $700 million to the Getty Trust on condition to expand the collection and show it to the public free of charge. The charming layout of the area with stunning views all the way to the Pacific soothes ones stay. The museum is located on the left side of Freeway 405 shortly before it joins Fwy 101.

The 3rd Freebee is the physical training that is as essential for maintaining a functioning body defense as the relaxation: *We can play tennis for free. Each community provides its citizens with some hard courts at leisure. Also, who can not find a suitable sleeping place, goes to Denny's. Denny's the American Diner is always open.*

These records were among my first literary outpouring in the form of a California trip report. As the first proof of performance it wandered, turning yellowing from drawer to drawer. My first book *Spirulina, das blaugrüne Wunder* based on my thesis about the microalga Spirulina and immune defense. Since then, I am enjoying the blissful process of writing and the good fortune to earn money with my hobby.

To Peter I said: Don't squander your talents live them! We create our reality. Imagine just what you do best. For me, it has worked. Mentally, I have organized readings and presented my books at the book fair. Peter grumbled: You can talk. You can write at any age. I'd have only fun, all day to buzz around the Nordschleife. Do you think anyone would give me old fart a dime to drive around *The Ring*? I replied, just imagine it every day! Unbelievable but true: A few months after I told my best friend to give his gray cells the creative training, he was offered a job as a test driver at Mercedes-AMG. For years, he had the opportunity to race through the *Green Hell*!

This principle of creating our reality makes us truly happy. A hobby can be a side job at first. I am in favor of trying everything that brings joy. Ultimately, our experience, is a true science. If, e. g., you want to spend the winter like us in North Africa, visualize the journey daily. Even if you are renting an RV first time and it is just a long holiday of four or five weeks.

A few years ago, Uschi Lenz generated a desire in me. She and her husband Jürgen, known among the campers as captain, explore South America for years with their SUV. That would also suit me. We know only Mexico, where we were on the lookout for rust-free vintage autos in the late 1980s. Now I dream to travel around Central and South

America. But instead embarking with the campers in Hamburg, trudge round European ports for four weeks and heading for Dakhla south of the Panama Canal, I imagine it to be like this:

We fly to California and buy a vehicle. With it, we drive to the Mexican border, take out additional insurance and look around in Central and South America. If we have enough, we sell the car or leave it at friends.

The two Franks leave their auctioned, self-developed Mercedes 911, a former radio car of the GSG 9, also in South America.

With us, it first evolved quite different. We ended up in Portugal. However, in my first year of retirement, we should be ready if no other life goal comes along. Everything constantly changes. Change is the only constant.

Visiting Bursins: Sandy & Sir Peter Ustinov

When leaving Michelstadt towards the Neckar valley we prepare ourselves mentally for the Christmas celebration with the Swabian children and grandchildren. We quickly pass Erbach, the community, which by the desire of many citizens and tourists would better unite with Michelstadt. When I completed my training as a medical assistant in Erbach, jokes about the warring cities were on the agenda:

Two women from Erbach talk about their evil neighbor who constantly beats up his wife. I would not put up with this. Do you know, from where she is? Well, from Michelstadt. Oh! Well, then she deserves it.

Down there in the paper mill, my father had worked in his youth as an electrician.
  So he had a short circuit current in his pants.
  Ha, ha! So you are telling lame jokes! A last glance wanders over the crest of Schönnen's willow slopes. In front of the sharply defined mixed forest sits enthroned the line keeper's house. The light brown-stone beams in the bright sunshine. The barren limbs of the flanking trees are frostily breathed on. In the warm period, the brownstone walls one can suspect at best behind a symphony of bushes and exuberant trees. That is probably one reason Günter Wallraff always rented it from my parents when he stopped in the Odenwald, talking about his investigative journalism. The brownstone house post 19 has a lot to tell!

During the war, there was a burlesque community of bombed-out relatives and friends. Until almost seventy years ago, when in the spring night with a grinding noise and a jolting clangor a tank of the U.S. Army rolled on. With its vibrating mass, it broke through the railroad gate and shook the house. Grandma hid the army coat of her still underage son, who had never come to serve due to illness and marriage leave. 50 years later, twelve Bosnians found here a new home. Why are thinking people always making war?

Silently we pass the magnificent stone railway bridge before Hetzbach. On the snowy height in Beerfelden, I sink deep into the seat. My face relaxes, and the eyes sink deeply into their sockets, the arms hanging limply. Whenever we leave, I feel completely detached and find the absolute peace in the movement. Peter teases me by saying, you forgot to mention that your grandmother has saved the viaduct. More than once I had reminded him in passing about how at the end of the war she could prevent blasting the imposing building:

When the soldiers were approaching, the resolute gate tender asked after their intent. The commander said; we have orders to blow up the viaduct. Are ye mad? The war is almost over yet. It is enough destroyed already.

The Americans will certainly not come by train. If you want to blow something, you may as well blow up the small Marbach bridge. The convinced man just did the latter.

In the past, almost every Sunday we visited Mother's sisters in Eberbach. Almost every time we passed the beautiful viaduct, Pa reminded us that it would not be there without Grandma and that she would deserve a medal. *In the spirit, I looked out the split windows of our VW Beetle on the colorful magnificent brownstone building. Uphill to Beerfelden driving, Pa intoned the song "If we climb to dizzying heights ..." and all together singing we drove to the summit cross.*

The hills with their cobweb fine ice crust glisten in the sun and make me tired.

Soon we'll come to the Malibu of the Odenwald. Yes, Peter and to *my red* house. Just before reaching the underpass towards the river of Neckar, it appears. As a child, I wanted us to move to **Eberbach**. In my mind, I hear my mother call. *Your red house, Marianne, we are almost there!* House was an understatement. The gelatin factory is the largest in the world. Every fourth ton of animal protein comes from this family operation.

Was it my mother's prophetic ability that she called it my red house? Well, I have nothing to do with it, but the great-granddaughter of the plant's founder Heinrich Koepff is my beautiful daughter-in-law. Michaela's relatives as well as my mother's live in Eberbach. Even she celebrates her birthday together with Doris Day and her daughter Marika celebrates on my father's birthday!

Brown dazzles the gentle waters of the stream. From fine rising mist, the sun conjures silky angel hair. The shrouded black-green hills of the Neckar valley and the hazy horizon seem to belong to another time. A feeling of infinity carried me away. Only when Peter asks about the passports I leave the island of the blessed. For the first time since the accident of our dog, we stay again at the service area of **La Côte**, just a few hundred meters away from Sir Peter Ustinov's grave. The entire film is unspooling again:

Peter wakes me shortly after 7:00 o' clock. In an angry tone, he says, you have to take care of your dog ... the bitch doesn't come when I call. As in a trance I put on my jeans and say: Why did you let her off the leash? In a remorse-tempered voice Peter answered, there was a guy with a boxer. He had let him walk back to the meadow. I detached Sandy, and the two have played with each other. Then the guy called his dog. I've also called Sandy, but she showed me this. He raises his middle finger.

I run around shouting. No curly white dog with black spots in sight. I cut cross country in the direction of the nearby village Bursins. In the distance, I spot ... It is taking a load of my mind. I get a wiggle on. Sandy, Sandy! As I get closer to the cemetery wall, I meet a tall black-haired woman. My delicate bitch turns out to be a well-fed Boxer mix. The warm-hearted French woman who leads another dark-brown four-legged friend on a leash seems to sense my sorrow. Her face expresses painful regret, when I ask after a border collie mix, le chien blanc-noire, and keep a hand on the height of my mid-thigh. While I caress her pets, she patters some opportunities where I could look for Sandy. When parting, she wishes me "Bonne chance."

In Bursins, I speak to an auto mechanic who is trying to start an old R4. He says, on the other side of the service area is a police station and offers to drive me. I hope to be able to reassure me through jogging and reject, but am pleased with the kind offer.

I get into the elevator, cross the car-track, go

down on the other side and walk past the petrol station to the police-building. What follows, I had dreamed of 1½ years before. At that time I advised my mother not to bind emotionally too attached to Sandy, she will be not getting much older than two years. Sandy lived from 27.11.1998 to 1.12.2000.

I ring, and a civilian officer comes to the door. I ask for Sandy. The man nodding says something in French, which I do not understand. However, the hand movement to the neck artery was too clear. He goes into the building and comes back with another officer. Sandy's red leather neckband in the hand, he looks at the tax stamp and asks, où est-ce que vons habitez? Half suffocated I breathe, Michelstadt. Saying oui he hands me Sandy's red, lined with ivory leather collar. Burning tears well in my eyes. I turn around and walk back to the camper. I quietly say; Sandy has been run over. She died instantly ... the head looks bad. The policeman asked if we want to have her. In minutes long solidification we sit there. Then Peter just takes off. I say nothing. A little later I mumble; we would have rather buried her somewhere in the forest. Now her body is in a black bag, and her soul body is with us. She will not understand why we do not notice her. We often only learn the hard way. However, this rule we have downed: On a roadhouse,

*under N O circumstances have
your four-legged friends unleashed.*

Doris Day had a similar experience as a teenager with her dog Tiny. Again, teardrops trickle down cheeks. Once more lumps choke in throats. We find no gas station, because it is Sunday. Contritely, Peter says; the spare can is empty. I say: As always well prepared! In Annecy, we finally find a gas station.

*On weekdays, you can fill up
at the lowest cost at supermarkets.*

We supply ourselves with some energy and joke during brunch on the great ski area with bare-branched sad-looking forests. In Beerfelden was snow, here no single flake. We regret our friend, who nearby suppose to enjoy her skiing holiday together with her children and friends. I say, 15 km from Chambéry and not a scrap of snow in sight. Poor Csöpi, this will be a New Year's Eve. We pack up and get the Hymer in gear. It goes steadily upward. Suddenly dies the day. Above us, fades shower thick gray. Leaden heavy snow falls on the windshield. The road has turned into rinse water. The wiper pushes the sticky wet in snail pace. Even at 15 miles per hour, Peter fears to slip at any moment. He says; if we get stuck here, then good night New Year's Eve in Marbella.

I say we could call Csöpi; she is only 20 km away from us, or a tower from Rumilly may have mercy with a member of the sister city. For more than forty years, Michelstadt builds bonds of friendship to the Savoy town.

Luckily we manage without a girlfriend and rescue service. However, I make a big memory knot in my gray matter: In the future, we skip the sneer and rest only after defeating a mountain range or after the descent.

Sour is not funny

On the circumvention of **Narbonne**, there are resting run-down 2CVs *two steam horses* on a giant junkyard. If Citroën 2CV owners lack parts, they can find them here. Wind turbines rotate at the exit of Port Novelle, also not far from the formerly Spanish city **Perpignan** in front of the background of the snow-covered massif of the Pyrenees. Environment and the economy are not contradictory. At the sight of the exquisite peak, I make a mental note:

*Fill up with plenty of drinking water.
One of the best is Montcalm, the tasty light
mountain spring water from the Pyrenees.*

Therefore, the first way in Spain leads us to **Mercadonna supermarket**. We supply us with plenty of Montcalm bottles (pH 6,7-6,9). The Moroccan spring waters, Sidi Ali and Sidi Harazem, are more expensive and contain many more minerals. The fewer inorganic salts are in the water, the better it cleans our body and the fewer deposition problems we have: such as Alzheimer's, arthritis, arteriosclerosis and stone formations. Minerals are best absorbed by the body if plants metabolized them through photosynthesis. We best obtain them from fruit, salad and vegetables!

In Portugal, we use **Cruzeiro** mountain spring water though it is not as light as Montcalm. It has a pH count of 6.9. Most spring waters worldwide are in the acidic range. The Portuguese Monchique mountain spring water is one of the rare alkaline waters with a pH of 9.5. However, it contains 1.2 mg fluoride, so I only mix it with the more acidic fluids. Recommended: after drinking cola (pH 2.5)!

Write to your elected representatives so we can inform us about the waters' pH-value!

The hissing and the smell in the chemistry classroom are vivid in my memory. However, from the teachings I have retained little more than acids color litmus paper red, bases dye it blue. Decades later, I learned during my studies in nutrition science, the importance of a neutral mixture of humors for our well being. Acidic food has to be neutralized with basic buffer so that the pH of the blood does not come too much in the acidic range. Who eats bread, pizza, hamburgers, hot dogs, chips, pastries and sweets, needs green stuff or soon no more comb! 70-80% of our food is better basic: cucumbers, zucchini, green leafy vegetables, dandelions, plantain and other things you need to find on flowering meadows away from traffic.

You wonder about my commitment? After the numerological point of view, I am a basic type 7 (cross total from birth, month and year). The sun is assigned as a planet, and it is to the manner born. Helmut Kritzinger writes in his book Numerology and partnership: *With 7/34, the discipline (Sun-Saturn) brings a sense of responsibility for one's behalf and all fellow humans. Their ideas about life (Uranus) are made readily available to others. This function can be as a medium or channel. The helpfulness connected with a heart for the problems of all fellow men predestine this type 7 early on for the role of a life consultant.*

Own knowledge I acquired through acid-forming foods, chemical drugs and X-rays. It weakened my Immune system. At age 10, I suffered senile cataract in both eyes, as I had already accumulated so many toxins and slag as with age 70.

France's idyllic, poplar-lined roads inspire me again and again. They remind me of the beautiful avenues, which gave my grandmother and me shade, when we marched to the line-keeper's lodge. The trees fell victim, like many others, to the racers. We stay in the charming fishing village of Méze. Peter gets a dozen oysters in the market hall. *I am not keen on the booger with fish taste.* Later an older American, who lives here disclosed that

the oysters in the shops at the street are better and not more expensive. The space in Méze with disposal & Water is free in winter.

We pass the winery Château Font des Prieurs in **Gabian**. The year before, we allowed ourselves 5 liters of organically grown wine on the return trip. Now we buy in **Le Boulou** two barrels of red wine recommended by Dieter and Ingrid. The ex-teachers traveling in a Flair are specialists when it comes to the le Rouge. They too know many hot springs in southern Europe. Ingrid has MS. After the bath, she gets better. The hot springs often locate in the vicinity of volcanoes. They help with skin diseases and muscle pain and have a soothing effect on depression or internal conditions. You can find them among others in places whose names begin with Fuente (= fountain).

A 53 ° C (127° F) hot spring you can find in Balneario de Fortuna, Murcia.
It helps with rheumatism and respiratory diseases. You can stopover here pleasantly.

Last year, we spent the night after our visit to the winery behind an oak scrub forest and enjoyed the splendid view of the powdered Catalan Pyrenees. You can stand overnight at the winery if the wine tasting comes off a little too intense.

At the border town of **Le Perthus**, the traffic jams more than usual. The crush as on the market of Timbuktu has to do with the increase at tobacco prices. Many Frenchmen stock up on coffin nails without thinking about the damage they cause on all organs over time. Perhaps the study of the States may deter some smokers. Result: The cigarette smoke can lead to blood, stomach, kidney and pancreatic cancer and carries an increased risk of suffering from eye diseases and blindness. Spirulina and Astaxanthin help lessen the risk.

Hookers and the karmic law

The approaching dusk covers the scurried landscape with melancholy. This year we notice the many prostitutes from the CIS countries, who come voluntarily or involuntarily to the West. My thoughts drift to Michel Friedmann, whose political program we miss. I like to mention him within the context of group reincarnation to explain the concepts of reincarnation and karma. Would it not make sense if those Nazis who in the early 40th recruited forcibly Polish and Russian workers for their munitions factories, now working as kidnapped ladies of pleasure, exploited by Jewish citizens?

If we always reincarnate to avenge us, may those who have been deprived of the most brutal way of their future like millions of Native Americans in their next incarnation are on the side of the barbarians. They want to learn how it feels to treat people worse than cattle. Such as in the shoes of Nazi officers who order to murder millions of Jews and thus annihilate life planning of as unique people at a single blow.

What will happen to the girls when they are no longer attractive enough to turn tricks? Can they take care of themselves, undergo training? Will they be sent back? Peter says, maybe they land in the Volga.

Why do people live in poverty and are exploited? The karmic law of cause and effect states: For every action a reaction follows. If I give something to others, I get it back with interest by any means. If I take anything from another, it will be taken me with interest. If we bring to mind of this law before any action, we will be always conscious of our actions. Then we would rather renounce a blow as it would hit us later in this life, or another, even stronger. We get everything back. An eye for an eye, a tooth for a tooth. When Jesus says that the once given a strike should also turn the other cheek, he says, that then goes off his karmic debt. The hereby Enlightened is then free from the wheel of karma. He no longer needs to atone for his sins. As he realizes that he has the attacker struck in another body in a past existence himself, he forgives him his blow. He asks him with turning the other cheek at once forgiveness that he has beaten him before. Alfira Weihe, the pediatrician who translated my book into

Russian, said when I mentioned reincarnation on the phone: I am a Christian, and therefore do not believe it. However, the early Christians were aware of the rebirth in another body! At that time, it belonged to the Christian doctrine. The churchmen took it out because humanity is allegedly not considered mature enough for the truth. It was all about exercise of power. The people are better to exploit, when they are afraid. The continuous fake pandemics also serve as scaremongering.

Just think about the above quotation of retaliation: Would it make sense without the reincarnation? We know from experience that some people all their life enrich themselves at the expense of others or harm others without legal consequences. Then there are those who care for others a lifetime but in the end, standing there all alone with no thanks. Would this make sense at all without any prospect of an equalizing justice in the next life? Therefore, an eye for an eye... or the sacrifice can only mean: We come back to either avenge or to turn the other cheek. First implies we reincarnate again and again in order to meet our karma. If we however renunciate on the revenge and forgive us and our fellow human beings, we are freed from the wheel of karma and hence from the fleshly life.

As long as we do not recognize the karmic law, the humanity problem persists: Always somewhere on earth terrible atrocities are committed in the name of revenge.
Again and again we return and participate in what some call a cosmic joke, many call it the earthly vale of tears.

I at times quote in my books Jesus, because, until the age of 12, I was used to preachings every Sunday in the New Apostolic church by my father or an uncle. These stored wisdom in my gray cells could as well originate from Buddha or any other spiritual leader.

On the coastal road N 340, not only many hookers waiting for johns are apparent. Also, countless clubs with their garish lights attract truck drivers, but at daytime, you hardly get it.

At the Ebro Delta, we are embraced by comfortable temperatures. No more fishermen at work, no more farmers in their fields. Even the usually lie in waiting officers of the Guardia Civil have quitting time.

Between Tarragona and Castellón, we fill in Vinaròs at Sebaco the least expensive fuel on this route.

Here, two surveyors still exert their plumb bob to gauge a new commercial zone. About a kilometer further on, we buy a battery at a Carrefour supermarket.

The coastal town Borriana south of Castellón offers a disused campsite with water and disposal.

We sleep calmly as in Abraham's bosom. On the highway, which is free to Valencia, we pass four pig transporters with crowded standing animals that can barely move. Shocked Peter shouts, take away all my sausages.

I say, simply buy no more. The poor pigs are transported through Europe to Morocco because the slaughter is cheaper there. An unimaginable stress! Torn from their usual environment, with strange animals squeezed in. Crashes an animal it is injured or killed by the kicking others. Schopenhauer said: "The world is not a piece of machinery and animals are not articles manufactured for our use. We owe the animals not mercy but justice."

We could stop the vicious excesses of agricultural policy and artificial price policy. We better prevent animal suffering for hefty premiums. We better boycott cheap animal products. If we reduce meat consumption and eat products from species' appropriate breeding, we protect the creature and collect less bad

karma and harmful substances. The daily feed of dairy and meat animals contain antibiotics for the prevention of diseases, among other toxins. Because of this and the harmful saturated fatty acids vegetarians suffer only half as often from cancer as carnivores. Also, with plant nutrition the resource water would less rapidly go downhill because producing meat requires 15 times more water than producing cereals. In 2025, every second human being will suffer from severe water shortage. Already, 10 million people a year are dying from the effects of contaminated freshwater (3rd World Water Council, Kyoto 2003).

Just thinking about Susanne and Kenny in Marbella, the cellular beeps. Kenny asks: Are you coming to New Year's Eve? Where are you? Peter says: 50 km from Granada. Kenny says: Then you'll make it today. No, it's too late, we'll stay somewhere after Granada. We'll see you tomorrow around noon. The receiver quality of our friend confirms Rupert Sheldrake's morphic field theory. According to it, there is a telepathic connection between organisms through space and time.

We spend the night in **Láchar** where our friend from Calpe had almost exchanged a Moorish castle against his villa in Austria. The deal failed. The owner wanted to switch even. KD wanted money on top. Since greed gets punished, I learned this with Peter often: the house in Austria was a loser.

Peter shows me the reddish brown washed colossus with the golden ornaments. He says the owner has another house in Jávea. He will now only go sailing. Good for him.

I was with Karl-Dieter when he inspected the castle, pretty spartan, he envisioned a modeling agency a la Star Search. He wanted to assign Toni Herner, as with his other residences, too, to equip the rooms with cozy sofas. In each bedroom, he wanted a Bang & Olufsen hi-fi and TV installed. I interpose: Each to his own. My dream would have less to do with media fuss. For me, it would be a health and cultural center.

The step from the donkey to the automobile occurred in many regions of southern Europe too fast. Car wrecks and prohibiting signs on motorway access with mapped tractors, bicycles, riders and pedestrians testify. We pass on using the freeway despite frequent jams between Fuengirola and Marbella. We campers barely get upset about congested roads because we are always at home and can just make a tea or have a bite to eat.

In La Cañada shopping center, we buy a magnum bottle of champagne. Peter shows me Manne's Snack Bar. That brings back memories: The obese father-in-law of the owner sold our cars in the late 1970s. Hugo had then gambled his car business on the casino. The amusing narrator always reminds me of a figure of Balzac's La Comédie Humaine, those captivating books that I all devoured in my youth. To each their own. Hugo would generate some laughs if I should eventually perpetuate the Frankfurt car dealers of the 1970s and 1980s.

On New Years Eve I help Susanne with her spaghetti Gourmet. Modified to our Gusto (excluding shellfish) you can find the recipe on page 79. The 1½ year old Jolyne runs with her bottle of cocoa and cereal around in the kitchen and enjoying life. Franco plays with the figures of a predator ship, which he flatly allied with those of the Seaworld visitors. KD is calling. He has an appointment with the German-speaking dentist in Marbella and asks if he can sleep a few nights at Kenny's with Corinna.

On Friday evening, we all sit around a wooden table in the kitchen. Pictures from Junior walk around. Susanne says to Corina; Tavo has your eyes. No, she replied, he has Karl-Dieter's green eyes. The latter drinks more red wine today, as we all are. A few of my brain cells are devoted to the truism: Money does not buy happiness or does he just want to dull toothache?

01-04: KD is sitting with Corinna at the breakfast table, his head resting on his elbows. He looks with swollen eyes. I say: You do not look happy. Are you eating enough fresh food, do you exercise enough? Corinna opens her eyes wide and snorts with raised eyebrows from a cubic meter of air. I state: So nothing. If you do not move your bones, they disappear, even the jaws. Eat crisp raw vegetables every day, and your dental problems are history. Acids attack the teeth. Green stuff is alkaline and neutralizes the acids. I know it from experience; as a kid I was more at the dentist than in the cinema.

Who does not move the bones or mandibles, suffers at some point from osteoporosis.

The lady of the house comes with a freshly washed blonde mane from the sleeping area. I go with her outside to perform the 5 Tibetans on the lawn. KD says, are you doing the humming top again? Susanne places the movie camera on the table, so that she can mimic the positions later. We just change from the bridge to the mountain, when Peter gets into the spirit of optimism. He wants to ferry quickly over to Morocco.

KD calls out, eh, if you want, I'll get you with your new book on TV. I say, oh, I do not know if that brings so much. I once presented my Spirulina books on prime TV, but the sale did not sooo much increase. Dismissively KD says, well, Spirulina, then the tone of voice switching to a promising one, the people are more interested in the supernatural. Yes but I did not even sell a hundred of Spirits in L. A., and Dr. Hittich will buy fifty thousand copies of my Spirulina book as a gift for his many customers. That's generous, but I still think if it is rightly organized ... let it be, I prefer to write, the hype is annoying me. Peter says; that goes with it; otherwise it's for the birds. I do not need anybody to tell me what I should do or not do.

KD and Kenny are artists in wheeling and dealing anything. When we still were among the traders, we only sold cars, new cars, convertibles and lastly antique ones. Our most famous cars were Yul Brynner's 300 SL Gullwing and Grace Kelly's 190 SL. But we more and more break away from desire, passion, consuming, void values of the world we have created. We currently practice letting go and temperance. That goes splendid with an apartment on wheels. We stand free, where we like it, alone or in groups and recognize: We do not need much to be happy.

On the way to the British enclave Peter says, we should visit KD on our way back and nail him to his proposal. I say, oh I don't know. Peter says, maybe that way we get our money back. I wish. Only imagine all our outstanding debts in a heap... we'll be set for life: Joâo, Julio, Schnitzler, Strott, Zimmerlein, Rost, the Jaguar, and Martin, the polo-playing playboy. How much he owes us, 150 grant?

Gibraltar, a small country and small world phenomenons

Driving through **La Duquesa**, we discover the roundabout that leads to the castle, where we usually spend a few days at the beach. The grounds on which once bustled 6-8 red cats, is now fenced.

We continue on the N 351 towards La Linea. The Rock of **Gibraltar** lies ahead. The barbed wire fence around the enclave propagates the usual dreariness. The cable car is again not in operation, but most visitors come anyway just because of the duty-free goods.

In 1998, we managed to cycle around the Monkey Rock in 3½ hours. Only in the tunnel we had to get off the bike and take the hill on foot. When we arrived back at the port, we saw a couple with two tiny dogs on leashes standing at the window of a boat dealer. They were familiar to me. Were they actors in a prophetic dream? About the dogs, I came in contact with the two. The conversation with Désirée, who gives body, mind and soul stimulating courses, brought a mutual acquaintance to light.

Peter pointed to a boat in the shop window and nonchalantly moved the for him vexing issue, which then landed at Robert Redford. He had a boat that was in the vicinity of theirs. But the meeting was arranged for me, because we were voila, on the old topic, as I said, I know the housekeeper of Robert Redford. She is a sannyasin. I met her often with my friend Anda. By the way, I was also at Hasya's house, the wife of the producer of The Godfather. She heads the Hollywood group of Sann ... Eh? I know Hasya well, Désirée interrupted my monologue elated with sparkle-eyes. Jung would have been delighted of this non-stop synchronicities. I ever suspect when I meet people at random; they might have been sent from spiritual helpers to assist me in my work. So I told Désirée of my psychic experience with my grandfather and why I would like to know whether I have relatives in USA. Désirée said: Go to Ellis Island and search under the name of the immigrants.

> *Small-world* stories or so-called coincidences count to these phenomena named by C.G. Jung. You may have already experienced such synchronicities: you work e. g. on a project and will suddenly mysteriously face a barrage of references and impulses. Or you will be suggested a topic as happened to me years ago after my acquaintance water researcher had died. All of a sudden, books, reports, announcements and E-mails on the subject of water turned up unexpectedly. So I could not help but to write a book about it. Our heavenly helpers are always ready to serve and support us. Let us follow our intuition, help comes to us always.

Yes, I know. Jocelyn Brando and two other friends from the film industry had already advised me to. But he has unlikely entered with the assumed name. He evidently took the name Victor later.

There you visit a small country and observe: The whole world is a village. Since I pay more attention to coincidences, they enrich my life. Do you feel sometimes when the phone rings that you know in advance who is at the other end of the line? Or you think about a particular person and shortly after he or she crosses our path. Or this way:

A few years ago, an inexplicable hounding drove us in 48 hours from Michelstadt to Calpe. We slept in the harbor next to the No Stopping sign! When in the morning we opened the door, a couple came around. The woman said: Erbach license plate, where are you from? Peter said, from Michelstadt. We too. I said I was a born Holschuh. She cried, oh, that's impossible. Yes, the laughter we can see it, Mrs. Holschuh. We know your mother. She once left her key inside her car at the cemetery. She rang and asked if she could call her daughter. Since you live in the area, my husband has driven her to you. Anyway, we are the Neumanns. I said, and we the Meyers.

I do not believe in coincidences. Could we have to tell us anything? Mrs. Neuman said:

Yes, that's strange, normally we never go hereabouts. Today, something has driven us in the harbor. Following a feeling I said, I have to do with health. Perhaps you have any problems, and I can revenge for your good deed. Amazed Ms. Neumann said:

I'm indeed suffering from back pain lately. See? You have come to the right place. Take 3 x 2 Spirulina tablets daily with a large glass of water. That's the amount a friend needs to be without pain. He's already been operated several times on the spine because it is badly worn from hauling heavy loads and smoking. Previously, he has also taken three times a day the strongest Tramal, also Valoron and Novalgin drops. On his birthday, I gave him a large glass of Spirulina. He has sorted the tablets into his drug box. As the big guns were empty, Werner has only taken this "Green Gold" and was surprised that he had no more pain.

It would be a blessing if we all took no chemical medicines.

You are right, and not only because of side effects. Two-thirds of the ingested drugs are excreted with the urine and pollutes streams and lakes. Through the water cycle, they come into our drinking water. That's awful. Yes, the engineer Thomas Junker from Erbach has built an award-winning mini sewage treatment plant. He wanted to trace a radioactive marked antibiotic substance. He has discovered that 93% of the drug will pass into the rivers!

The episode ended in Calpe with the handover of a glass with Spirulina tablets. A few months later Mrs. Neumann told me: I was feeling much better soon. My daughter now takes Spirulina regularly, too.

We register synchronicities as strange coincidences. Could it be we follow an impulse

from within and stage them ourselves after an inward urge? Do we communicate telepathically with each other? Have we orchestrated this meeting? Or do spiritual helpers arrange things and push us on our spiritual path?

01-6: Arriving in La Linea, immediately follows the usual procedure in obtaining duty-free coffin nails in Gibraltar, sometimes with the scooter, sometimes on foot. Then we take the opportunity to inline skate on the buttery soft asphalt. Until it is too dark to pay attention to the dangers that the ground can hide. In the previous year, a Hanoverian bus driver got a flat tire on a capped iron rod. After digesting his mishap, he was, however, amazed at how inexpensive and fast a nearby workshop mounted a spare tire.

Ferry ride and entry

Next morning, the same procedure. Otherwise, I have to persuade Peter to walk, but to the duty-free enclave he cannot come fast enough. Fortunately, he was able to give up the volatile toxic mixture. It contains arsenic, ammonia, cyanide, formic acid, formaldehyde, carbon monoxide, methanol, nicotine, phenol, nitrogen oxides, and 3000 other toxins.

Driving towards the harbor, we turn left to N 351 towards Algeciras until exit (Salida) 112 Poligono Palmones. After the second roundabout, behind Carrefour Parking we reach the agency of the STA Shipping & Transport.

There are always several campers there. It is after 10:00 a. m. We do not know when the next ship leaves. In the agency, I ask two young women for the group rate. Peter goes to the camper to get the vehicle registration. Prices have gone up around €33 from last time. Now the return ticket costs per camper and two persons 219, group rate 199. Juan Carlos shows up. I ask about the increased prices. The boss looks at his watch and says: It is now 10:20. The ship goes at 11:00. If you agree to € 210...

I say okay, give the girl my last year's boarding pass so that she can transmit the data of the vehicle. I give her €250 and change the rest in dirham. To change more is not advisable.

In Marocco, the exchange rate is better.

Peter walks towards me. With an am-I-good-or-what-twinkle I say, all cleared, we must hurry. The ship goes in a good half hour. Now everything goes pretty fast: Shopping (tips in the appendix), back to the port (Puerto Northe). At 10 to 11:00 we rush as the last vehicle on the ship, which takes about 2½ hours. The speedboats need only 35 to 45 minutes. They are just leaving ahead of us. The Trasmediterranea ferry with its open bow looks like an attacking shark. With magnificent sunshine and calm seas we take off shortly before 11:30 It is a busy ship operating around the Ape Rock. I sit at one of the white plastic tables and write while Peter strolls, holding his binoculars, from one side to the other. Occasionally he snaps behind a departing ship.

From the noise, swings and alternating writing and looking up I feel queasy. Despite calm seas, the ups and downs are enormous. The ship is filled up to the brim and is scary-deep in the water. Where are the life jackets on deck? Though the question haunts my gray cells, I laugh inwardly about it. I'm not afraid of the departure from this life. But the thought of how the dying process would be this time, creeps in from time to time. It would be ideal, just to go over in bed or to die standing; like a tree felled by lightning or mowed down grass. Who needs an agonizing struggle for survival? I think of an acquaintance with the near-death experience by drowning. She said: It was not that bad. The feeling that you cannot breathe holds on just a moment.

We go down into the ship body. The line of people indicates that the entry formalities for parties are conducted. Leisurely sliding on the ferry to the western entrance to the Strait of Gibraltar. The sun coats the white city with a gentle glow. We are heading towards a futuristic landing stage: Tangier's Special Entrance. The monster opens its mouth and spits out the vehicles. A civilian police officer checks the passports of the departing vehicles. We follow the others to customs clearance. The process still leaves lots to be desired in terms of coordination. A trilingual leaflet would be beneficial.

In the car, just fill out the green entry declaration for vehicles and wait for an official in a blue uniform to collect them and check your passports. When he returns with the stamped paper, one of the traveling persons in the car must go with the passports to the issued police control.

After all our repeated entries, we are not taken in by hectic aid volunteers. They try to rip the papers out of newbie's hands. All want to earn a few dirham. It's much quieter than before.

We leave the port building, keep left and on the light, turn right towards Rabat and airport.

A few hundred meters further we refuel at the Marjane supermarket diesel (gas oil) for 56Dh per liter (today it is about 85Dh). We buy fruit, vegetables, fresh goat cheese and spicy black olives. Heaps of Olives, nuts, dates and figs invite you to try. People seem to be in a better mood than before. The reforms of the young king seem to grip. Last year we already noticed a change. Five years ago some children responded aggressively, if they did not get any candy. Since Mohammed VI, named *M6*, urged the population via TV not to harass tourists, there is peace. The literacy rate of men may soon be in decline. Despite nearly a quarter of the state spending on education, 43% of the men and 69% of the women are not able to read and write. Projects are launched like the one the beach chairs seller Mustafa supports. He does not need to pay taxes because he is funding a boarding school together with other entrepreneurs, in which about 200 children of the area are housed. Mustafa talked to us about these projects when he sat with us and a girl who came to beg. He gave her 2Dh but immediately advised her to stop begging and go to school.

Truck drivers flash to welcome us as guests or to warn us of controls. Peter inserts an audio cassette of Fleetwood Mac. His former booze buddy from Malibu puts his shoulder to the wheel. We drive through a small alley. On the left appears a lake, on the right the Atlantic Ocean. A herd of goats grazing at the roadside. Young dromedaries cavort on the beach. A car driver flashes. Peter is preparing to pass. I say, wait, I think the cops are close. This time Peter listens to my advice, but a blink later he says annoyed: Now even the trucks are passing us. I raise my hand warningly. Seconds later a bus races towards a truck on the opposite lane. Shortly after this truck and a car park at the roadside, where the cops deal with the traffic offenders.

Some campers stay for a while in beautiful **Asilah**. Again we are warned by an oncoming bus driver of a police check. Peter has enough. He heads to the highway. However, the route turns out to be a detour. There is no car. On the emergency lane, we meet a young cycling Moroccan. After exiting in **Larache**, we find 1 km on the right side the famous roadhouse **Aire de repos**. On the hospitable terrain, you can easily refresh under the roaring waters of the free showers. In the evening, we enjoy a delicious soup and other local dishes.

Hassan II founded this free overnight accommodation. The father of "M6" offered it as a gesture of hospitality for locals and visitors, as well as the Aire de repos Malabata in Tangier and the Aire de repos Kenitra in Kenitra North.

Almost all campers enjoy the delicious Harira soup with chickpeas. They bring in their pots. Including flat breads, it costs 20 Dh, that is about €1.80 per pot. We meet Christina and Hartmut from Lübeck. They are part of a guided tour. I hit on the idea of carrying out wellness tours, including Reiki, Yoga, GIE-Water and Spirulina for the participants. In the morning, we enjoy copious showers and hair wash. A thick bundled up young Moroccan woman lets the water run for me until it squirts out hot. Hadija says: Malade. She indicates chills. Her forehead is lukewarm. I say: I later will transfer Reiki. She looks quizzical. I make signs on her forehead and roll conspiratorially with the eyes. When thinking the word Voodoo slips from my lips aloud, because I'm looking for a similar approach. Hadija laughs with a complicity nodding. In Morocco, the belief in magic, witchcraft and all sorts of healing is common, although it contradicts the pure teachings of Islam. In the camper, I start immediately with the distant healing. Later I see her walking by. I call, Hadija, Ça va? Malade fini? The beauty beams at me from a distance.

Around 11:00 a. m., we leave the oasis of hospitality. Some visitors enjoy it for a week. I'm soaking up the flying by eucalyptus forests, nurseries, olive groves, fruit ranches and stork's nests. Peter spots a souped-up vehicle of the Dakar Rally in the for him rather monotonous plain of the Moroccan North. I adore nature; he loves technology, I smell the fragrance of everything growing; he likes the stench of consumption. People often ask me why we are together despite conflicting interests.

We choose the route via Casablanca and Marrakech. It is less far, and the roads are better. However,

if you visit Morocco for the first time,
better take the attractive coastal road.

You can see more of the country and people. Farmers often still plow with odd-toed ungulates hitched up before the plow. Strawberry and tomato growers have taken over the Spanish habit of using plastic covering. Moroccan agricultural workers are lucky if allowed to work in Spain. At the last crossing, a strawberry picker told us he earns in Lepe in one month, what he'd had in Morocco in six.

Around Rabat dominate pine forests and cacti. As on Ibiza: red soil. Ibiza, youth, I remember an exercise against flabby cheeks and double chin. I rarely remember to rebuild the tissue. Just as we can enlarge our muscles in the gym, we can do it with isometric: I push the lower jaw forward and keep tense 5 seconds, release. Rest 10 seconds. Repeat ten times. Against wrinkles above the upper lip, push the upper jaw forward and flex to the side as if you want to reach the ears of each upper lip side. For me, it works better against sleeplessness. The *lion* in Yoga helps too.

In a usual police control, the officer is waving friendly. Tourists are rarely stopped. At best, if they manage to take a pic of a bribery. In the fast lane, the passenger of a car talks with some men sitting on the loading area of the truck. It's a daring demeanor, especially since the brake lights of the truck fails. No less dangerous are the stunts of the vegetable hawkers who trade on the emergency lane. We constantly need to watch out for cross-pedestrians or people who are trying to get a ride. Usually, hitchhikers pay the driver the cost of a bus ride. On the freeway tollbooth, a good-humored young Moroccan displays two rows of dazzling white strong teeth. Before Settat the freeway ends. A lovely palm avenue runs through the city. 125 km off Marrakech, we drive through an idyllic mountain underpass, as the train rushes off above us. At the road-side, young men offer wild green asparagus and fresh eggs from free-range hens. An old man holds a chicken tied together by the feet towards the road users. Apparently the fowl did not agree with the freedom. The trade regulates itself. Meters thick cacti rows define the fields, so animals are not about to trample the crop. Formerly, I pierced my big flower-pots with little cacti to convince our tomcat Foxi of the advantage of the litter box.

Déjà vu in Marrakech

The sloping Atlas throttles the drive. The sky swallows the last light. A sparkling sea of Marrakech's lights shimmers through the trees.

We pay attention that we do not miss
the campsite 15 km from the royal city.
After the gas station, we turn right.

While I am preparing dinner, Peter sets the automatic satellite dish. The usual whirring, suddenly it stops dead. It did not move one more nanometer. We are once again without TV. Last year, the Oyster gave up the ghost on our return trip in Gibraltar.

The morning sun sticks her pale arms tentatively towards us. Peter putters around on the roof, attracting Günther. As always, when there is any fine-tuning going on, neighbors are there to help or learn. The retired health practitioner lends us a wrench. With it, Peter screws the dish off.

In the turmoil of the residential city's one

million inhabitants, we are careful not to drive through one of the arched gates into the Medina. Last year we were mousetrapped exactly there and had to leave the old town which is surrounded by a twelve-kilometer long wall on the one-way street in the opposite direction. Therefore, we give the World Heritage cultural site a wide berth, spare our nerves and head for the

Parking area of the famous almost 850 years old Koutoubia Mosque

around the corner. The police seem to keep seized cars here. The guard demands Dh40 and takes cheeky grinning the 30 Peter holds out to him since last year it only did cost 30.

The *Red Pearl of the Orient* with its typical Berber character is one of the most beautiful cities of the Maghreb and Morocco's *secret capital*. In the Medina charms the colorful souk or suq.

The market is an important part of Oriental life as a site for commercial, labor and meeting.

Visitors can watch the creation of goods all the way up for sale. In cities, it is a permanent establishment. In the country, there are only weekly markets. The dyers' market is the attraction. The Almoravids took advantage of the former caravan storage area as troops base from which they conquered the whole country. From the following Almohads, there are only remnants of buildings because the advancing sultans always ensured full employment: They destroyed the palaces of their predecessors and chose to build their own.

During the colonial period, Pasha Glaoui El ruled the city. After the invasion of the French in 1912, he worked with them and procured advantages. When King Mohammed V. ascended the throne in 1956, it was made with the power of the Pasha. I am impressed how the grandfather of the present King M6 responded to the Nazis' asking to hand over the Jews. He supposedly said: There are no Jews in Morocco but only Moroccans.

The hodgepodge of different people is confusing. However, in conversations with locals we notice that they take the nativity of their families very seriously.

After brunch, we change €100. Pocketing the money, an old beggar woman with black tooth stumps slips through the door. On the way out, Peter brushes her yellow flowered robe and says, give her something. Instead of the usual dirham I place a 5Dh coin in her hand. Darkish-rimmed eyes shine overjoyed.

We plunge into the throng of the souk, starting on the north side of the Place Djemaa el-Fna, where once the heads of the executed were impaled. At a textile merchant in the premise white robe did passes as a nightdress, back home, Peter asks for the price of a Moroccan flag. The scene is familiar to me. Had I dreamed it? Peter says: Trop cher. The man with the white cap on the glassy bald head turns and rummages in his bales of cloth. This time was not a déjà vu after a prophetic dream: The dealer places, like five years ago, a red cloth with woven green five-pointed stars on the counter. Exactly this fabric we bought at the time, to protect us against aggressive attacks. Today we use it mostly on holidays as a table-cloth.

We wander around crisscrossing poultry, olive heaps, coppersmiths, past carpet dealers, wool dyers, woodcarvers. Surrounded by leather, jewelry and carpet market the crowd got to us, too much to digest. Just out!

We flee from spice dealers and quacks on Rahba-Kedima Square, where many black slaves were auctioned off, at the slave market for centuries.

Asking for our way to the Koutoubia, after what feels like 3 hours, the minaret shines in

the distance. The sun still sprays its sparks like an oven on us.

In the late afternoon, we stroll to the Djemaa el-Fna Jemaa and indulge ourselves in a glass of freshly squeezed orange juice for 2Dh. Dozens of young Moroccans offer the delicious drinks at the booths that line the busy square. When crossing the site of the colorful jugglers and barkers, we struggle our way through the crowd of nomads from the desert and people draped with cameras from around the world. We escape from self-appointed guides, beggars and water sellers. Next to the entrance of the souks we slip through the door of the Café Argana. On the first-floor terrace, we get a table in the front row and order two Moroccan whiskey. As such the Moroccans refer to their national beverage mint tea. We hear scraps of English conversation. Suddenly Peter says: Here we are sitting ducks for terrorists. Annoyed at the evil fellow who must have possessed him to undermine our trust, it takes not long for me to urge on leaving. It's not fear of death he awakens in me, but I cannot avoid imagining an assembly of shattered arms and legs in front of my mind's eye. Were these already premonitions?

On 4-28-2011, a bomb left in a bag killed 17 people, mainly European tourists, mostly young Frenchman. The historic café on the square of the juggler was destroyed, more than 20 people were injured. The authorities assumed an attack of the Al Qaeda terrorist network. Al-Qaeda denied this. In Wikipedia, I read about rumors via remote internet blogs that the attack was not carried out by islamist terrorists. The modus operandi was incongruent with Al-Qaeda or Al-Qaeda methods. The remotely ignited bomb points to militant groups in state or para-state organizations. The rumors came up that it was a plot by the government to appease the protesters of the Arab Spring.

In the midst of the instrumental sound and hubbub mix-up of the square, I feel safe. Above everything, like a bubble, inflates the excited murmur of the guests, sitting on the benches in front of the long tables of the food stalls. The aroma of cumin and coriander, reaching my nostrils, attracts to feast. We sit down on the bench of a steaming cook-shop, which competes with the many other mobile cooking stations. The chief cook has a bunch of a coriander herb clamped to his ear. All bearded men he calls Ali Baba and he praises his treats loudly. Opposite us, on a long folding table, sit four Berber women. Chatting, they feast on vegetable dishes. We ordered lentil soup, fried eggplant and spinach. Olives, tomato-onion sauce and pita bread we get to the place setting. Soups and vegetable dishes cost 5Dh. I say to the unveiled women: The Arabic word for gays, Sem(m)el, is in our language a bun. No respond. Many Berbers do not understand Arabic. We laugh about veiled belly dancers. The foolish mode and awkward movements reveal the men. We dig through the crowd. A hand skims my butt. Shortly after a repetition of this instance. It occurs to me that I already had experience with the hands-on type of Marrakech men years ago. I make a mental note to buy a hooded coat. After all, who does not appear as a tourist, has peace from gropers, touts and water-carriers. In their red costumes and huge hats, draped with bells, the latter determine the overall picture of the place. The dancers also shine in bright red robes, where tassels bob up and down. Passionately and spirited as Cossacks they swirl over the intended place for them. The snake charmer lures with insistent sounds of his clarinet the copra from the basket. Two Moroccans look in his direction. He buckles down to charm them as well, or the hedge-hogs, sitting in their pockets in front of their purses. I mime disinterest, not to be asked to pay up also. I see from the corner of my eye as the cobra sways back and forth as it rises in a trance. The sound of kettle drums, reed flutes, and other woodwinds have a meditative effect. I feel like I take off slowly. Only marginal, I perceive the exotic shacks. They seem like a framework for the presentation of acrobats and musicians. A few women cheerfully warble the zagharit, for the successful performance of the fairy tale-teller. I think of the Gulf War. At the time, often a similar scene flickered over the boob tube: Muslim women expressed their joy with the shrill tongue voicing. I felt strange about this, since I had no contact to their peers. We only develop understanding in dealing with people of other cultures. At the huts there are fragrant rose water, ointments, even used dentures, dried lizards, paws, skins and indefinable brews. They are supposed to heal everything, from the infertility of women to the gout of old men.

On the way back to the camper, we struggled through countless people and vehicles. Only from afar I perceive the roar and horns. Peter pulls the camera. Gently, I say, no, only check it out. Was that I was speaking? Suddenly I feel like floating on clouds like after my fire walking. As in ecstasy, I drift among an increasing number of young people. I dodge

donkey carts, mopeds and horse-drawn carriages and suspect that Peter did not follow me. I watch as he repeatedly ignores me in the crowd. Finding things is not Peters thing. I cross again the Mohammed V and walk towards him. From the minaret of the Koutoubia, the muezzin calls the faithful to prayer. The light of the setting sun makes all the buildings appear in time-honored splendor. The passers-by are strolling in the cool twilight hour on a wide sidewalk. They were mainly wearing wool white, brown and black djellabas and radiate dignity. The western clothes under the long Arab robes do not disturb the devotion.

Suddenly I am in the spell of the murmuring crowd in a solemn evening mood and feel in this surrealistic ambiance as protagonist of a monumental film. Flushed away by the waves of the goings-on, I am beside myself with happiness. Couldn't it be always like this! Why is it so difficult for many people to tolerate their contemporaries with different ethnic backgrounds, other artistic, spiritual and moral values or a different faith?

Jesus, who was appreciated by Mohammed, advised us to find happiness in and to trust ourselves. We better approach only the truth! In all nations, much knowledge has been accumulated. We just need to separate the wheat from the chaff, the truth from the dogma. We know by our gut feeling how to treat each other perfectly. And we know if something is the ideal of creation or does not match. We better trust our inner voice! It bids or forbids, regardless of benefit or pleasure.

We all have a conscience, conscientiae, which we have to follow. Must the creation to be changed? No! We better discipline ourselves and live in harmony with it. We have no right to prevent others from living according to the ideal of creation. Native Americans and Aborigines were despised as savages, enslaved and exterminated. They did not live by the Bible and prefer to trust their channel to the celestial beings. They did not share the colonial ruling view of the country, its animals and plants. But the main driving force for the genocide was the greed of their captors. The history of mankind is based on exploitation, subjugation and bloody reactions. With the blood as a factor, we approach the fundamentalism, which in turn leads to fundamentalism. Crusades, holy wars, never will it be possible to overcome the evil by something other than through patience and tolerance. We have a choice! And our actions have consequences!

We are an energy field whose movement has an echo in the entire universe, for which we are responsible, and we have earned. We are not victims of fate, but get the echo of our exerted free will to feel.

To act according the principle of an eye for an eye, a tooth for a tooth, can not be the true thing. Our determination is to learn to forgive over many incarnations and develop good will. All the great religions and philosophies assume in the origin of their doctrine the following: The cycle of transition from the spiritual into the material world and vice versa, is necessary. In contrast to churchdom, the doctrine of reincarnation is also known to Christianity. In the V. Ecumenical Council in Constantinople (553), then again in the Council of Lyons (1274) and the Council of Florence (1439), the church condemned them vehemently. Their followers were persecuted and often executed as a lesson on self-determination of the people would undermine the authority of the Church. When Jesus taught, it needed no temple to salvation but only the good will of every individual, this means the worship is service to others. Early Christianity, the Hindus and Buddhists centuries before Christ believed in reincarnation. And we would do well to reengage ourselves to this belief. Because:

Should we expect one day to live again on earth in another body, we'd better treat her and her inhabitants a good deal better.

Why should we not reincarnate? It would be just and logical. Tulips come again and again, grow onions and multiply, from caterpillars rise butterflies, why should the recurrence in another body be a greater miracle?

Also, many psychotherapists and psychiatrists prove that their patients under hypnosis remember past lives, and they are even often able to verify them. We reincarnate until our goodwill takes us to the longed-for final enlightenment. Then we accept the profound truth in the words of love thy neighbor as thyself and practice it. So we share our gifts, our respect, our consideration. We offer what we have; we give our essence, our nature. Devotion we all can give, even the poor. Especially parents better remember: Love is more important than money.

The scientific world has emphasized that, on principle, nothing present can turn into a non-existence. Therefore, why should our consciousness cease to exist? We live subsequently after the event of death without interruption. The self, soul or spirit comes into being and lives with the biological body. Consequently, after the event of death it continues to exist in a new form of existence. According to the environment in which it is located, it continues life in this world or in the Hereafter, which one is inseparable from the other.

01-08-2004: From the parking lot of the Koutoubia, we turn left to Mohammed V and then go straight, pass wrought iron pedestals on circuits up to the sign pointing straight to Casablanca, Agadir and left to Essaouira. At the exit of the town, the usual police check. The officers are waving us to pass. On dead straight, in the tar luster flickering street we pass cheerful young people in western wear. Before us lies the majestic High Atlas with a spiderweb fine sugar crust covering. The white powdered peaks glisten in the midday sun. In the channels (queds) lots of river stones, but not a single drop of water. From the curve, a white Peugeot hurls at us. Fortunately, the road edges are wide. But on the gravel the Hymer shakes critically. Peter says: We must again soon control the screws.

Gorgeous blossoming of almond trees. 128 km before Agadir it's going downhill. We can still one more time enjoy the splendid mountains of the High Atlas. The snowy peaks are coming closer. 99 km before Agadir a loaded truck with bales of straw touches us. The towering high matter remembers of a captive balloon. Uneasy, I wonder about the passing marvel of loading technique and think of a picture book with wheelers out of the ordinary. Even carts and motorcycles are often packed that they are three to five times higher and wider. Below the snowy mountain range, green argan trees are in razor sharp contrast to the red earth. In the area around the place Argane, street vendors offer the precious argan oil in yellow plastic bottles. The pharmaceutical industry uses it in ointments against eczema. Internally helps fructo-oligosaccharides (FOS), best in some aloe vera juice. Argan oil is extracted from a women's cooperative in a laborious process. The goats climb the trees to eat the fruit when the dry soil no longer provides much food.

We pass a reservoir: a silent witness to the global problem of water shortage. On a Japanese pickup truck, a two story self-made structure jiggles in the curve. An injured mutton strives for balance. In any left turn, his leg slid off the dilapidated paneling. Again we pass a van with a castrated sheep. The feast of mutton is imminent. 38 km before Agadir we leave the beautiful world of mountains behind us. The tachometer indicates 3,500 km we have driven.

My mom calls: Have you heard about the earthquake in Tehran? Yes, the Iranians better move their capital to an earthquake-poor area. If Tehran shakes as much as Bam, there will be millions of casualties. Ma says: I was at my tenants. Nushin has worried about her relatives. I said: What, Nushin is from Tehran? I thought she was from Tel Aviv. I hope she's not annoyed. In the book, I've let her come from Israel. Well, paper doesn't blush.

In my mind's eye the quake from 01-17-94 passes by, one of the strongest in the seismological history. Far fewer people would die if houses were built as in California. We lived in Little Tel Aviv of the Valley, about 700 meters from a seismological station. Experts from India, Australia and other countries marveled at the low damage in our area, especially since they measured much higher jolts than officially stated. The powerful earthquake that rattled at 4:31 as an express train through our bedroom, was estimated to be less than 7. Had it been correctly classified as over 7, Uncle Sam would have had to help us more financially by law. Even so, the Northridge quake was one of the costliest disasters in the last 30 years. It destroyed 11,000 buildings. Fortunately, there were only 60 deaths. Many of shock or heart disease had succumbed. In stone houses, thousands would have died.

Second home *Banana Village*

The starting point of all journeys within Morocco lies ahead. The port city of Agadir with its approximately 650,000 inhabitants is growing rapidly since its almost complete destruction in 1960. Not only we are magically drawn to earthquake areas. According to the motto no risk, no fun. But what is so appealing? The climate and the good-humored people!

On the west of the three parallel main streets, the Boulevard Mohammed V, we pass an older cyclists. He rests his hand on a young man's shoulder on a moped to participate in the PS. We stopped at the traffic light while next to us, a white car passes at bright red, despite the policeman's whistling and wildly gesticulating. But the metal box scorches further up the mountain. The police officer accepts it with composure.

Below us, the largest fishing port in Morocco spreads out. Here, sardines are canned and loaded on cargo ships together with oranges, bananas and other agricultural products from the Sous Valley. The crimson sun approaches the sea. The waves splash incessantly against the rocks. In Aourir, better known as Banana Village, we turn left after the bridge in the direction of the qued. Before we reach the dry river bed, we go right into the walled entrance. For the equivalent of €1, we can fill up the fresh water tank. It is a delight how nice the young people interact with the elderly! The youth, who fills us the water, calls smiling, bonjour madame, stretches out his hand through the window and asks how I am. Bon! Merci. Ça va? With that, my French almost exhausts. My preadolescent senile cataract stopped me from taking up voluntary subjects. Anyone who has ever read a single book page with a thread-counter knows what I mean.

When we got water five years ago, this young man was 12 years old. His siblings were always running out of the house when campers showed up. We had nothing sweet, so he gave the smallest girl who had not yet learned to tolerate her frustration, a candy. This experience brought me close to my childhood: At the beginning of the 50s, I grew up like that. Since our neighbors had it not better, and television had not aroused needs yet, I didn't miss anything. In the same apartment building also lived a sensitive boy. For me, Rolf Broich was a role model. Once, when I had lost all my marbles playing with older children, he reached into his pocket and held out his. My sense of justice would not let me take them, but by his offer, he rose in my respect. My brother's best friend has enriched our lives only briefly. He moved with his family to Hürth-Köln, leaving behind a sad boy.

Kindness and sensitivity, today are hardly mediated values. However, only in the deep feeling is the real experience of the human spirit. It triggers mental energy waves which manifold intensify. Currently, by our feeling, we are strengthening resignation or anger. The human mind may not be aware that feelings of envy or lack stimulate similar thoughts. Due to the connection to the power of the universe, through the law of attraction, our spirit has an impact on the world. We thus take responsibility. Therefore, we better strive for pure willing, virtue and justice. If we let allow our inner wisdom to guide us and change what is dishonorable, we get everything out of us, what we have to offer and get on ascending!

We could start at once with gender equality. The young man doesn't seem to act, as some Muslims represented in books. But the experience reports of abused women are frightening and humiliating. Muslim women and girls often envy their goats and donkeys because their husbands and brothers beat and offend them less. Many women also expect that they kill their female newborns. A harrowing life story is that of Souad from the West Bank. She was doused by her brother alive with gasoline and set on fire. What had she done wrong? She fell in love with a young man from the neighborhood. He deceived her during the sheep herding. He promised to marry her. But when she was pregnant, he didn't show up anymore. *She such has dishonored her family!* Brutality against the female sex is everywhere. Not always, it has to do with religion and tradition. But especially in followers of Mohammed the misconception has deep roots that men are superior to women and could do with them what they want. The tragedy is also that parents view their children as possessions and often marry them as children against their will. The Turkish-German sociologist Necla Kelek opens our eyes to this modern slavery in the interior of Turkish life in Germany.

In the gorgeous lilac dawn of the evening, the Hymer rumbles past the cemetery towards Devil's Rock. The support bearing squeaks critically. We need to order a new one via ADAC. Luckily we have a writ of protection.

The German, Madame Sigi, Sigrid Gratz leads an ADAC site, in Agadir, 24, Rue Mokhtar, close to the campground.

In the cupboards, it rattles and shakes. We discover the F 911 truck of Uschi and Jürgen, with whom we shared for two weeks this rugged scenic stretch of beach in the previous year. Again we enjoy as a foursome the view of the blue-green Atlantic. In fountains, the water splashes from the craters. Here we like it better than on *The Plate* that is divided into *Wrinkly City* and *Hymer 1 to 3*. Uschi says Willi and Gerti are also there. They are right in the throng. I know we have texted us. Tomorrow we'll roam to the crowd.

01-09: After a hearty brunch, we walk along

the beach to *The Plate* to visit the Vienna couple. 1998/99 we had been with them in the *Cacti*, nursing our puppies born in the nearby canyons. All of a sudden the images reappear:

Sandy, with her mother frisking, and I too, completely merged in maternity: With a light sleep and first-time hot flashes, I watched over the puppy's bladder. Dancing hormones, heart expanding inner radiance. My wrists were suffering from tendonitis from lifting the whelp. Out, in, dozens of times a day. Kept me from indulging in the here inexpensive sport where you hit the ball with a stick into a hole and get allocated a caddy, who appreciates golf considerably more than you.

Sindi greets me with wet kisses. She had at that time a lot of care needed. Fleas and other parasites besieged in droves her fur. I imagine Sandy immaterially with us. Near the Austrians are Gottfried and Gisela. They come to welcome us. And again vivified the past:

Between the campers of the two Saxons and the Clou of Loni and Karl of Upper Bavaria, we had barricaded ourselves in the almost 1000 km southerly UN city Laayoune behind house walls. Three long days the wind howled over our heads and put a yellow cover over houses and cars. Tons of sand swirled through the air burned like pinpricks on the skin and ate its way through the smallest cracks of our Hymer. Since then, it poses the honors as timeless souvenir. I learned to appreciate the symbol of oppression: The veil protects against wind, dust, odor or fumes and hides wrinkles. I could only read by candle-light. The yellowish cover prevented the power of the sun, so the solar cells didn't collect any juice. Then, these pestilential flies! Fortunately, Loni's procedure for getting rid of flies helped: We did not even have to kill them. They drowned themselves in a kamikaze dive. Peter filled a jam jar with plenty of dish-washing liquid and water and kept the fatal liquid at a distance of half an inch from the ceiling, where the insects preferred to stay. They hopped all by themselves in the glass. At once poured out and thrown outside, the flies even bobbed up again.

Before the dust storm was raging, we were right on the beach next to the property of the Governor. From there, each morning trotted a rather dimwitted one-year-old male dog and played with a wild bitch and our puppy. I observed how clever she was with her three months already. The two larger dogs were fighting over a bone. The brawny male was burying it and watch over it. The blonde tried to steal it. Sandy played the disinterested. Suddenly she ran to a three-yard remote location and dug up as insane so that the paws almost smoked. Both dogs approached curiously. Shortly thereafter, six paws flew through the air. When Tom, Dick and Harry were in their element, with an imaginary upraised middle finger, Sandy trotted calmly to the point where Bully had buried the bones. She pulled it out and tackled it. The brown and the blonde conspecifics trotted taken aback to her, admitting defeat. How can a puppy already be that smart? Sandy saw the light of day on my birthday, two months after my father had left his bodily shell. Therefore, I fancied that my old man gave us a course in dog love. He would have liked to have a four-legged friend himself but because of my brother's night job, he never had asked for a barking one.

In Laayoune, we had the opportunity to see an ordinary residential house from the inside. Loni, Karl, Peter and I were invited to a couscous dinner. The hosts were an unequal couple with a two-year-old son. She was 25 or so, and he was at my age, but had hardly any teeth left. There are no beds. They sleep on colorful blankets that during the day serve to sitting. In the morning, they fold them and stack them with pillows on the walls above the other. Particularly impressive is the automatic wash facility: Through a square opening in the hall ceiling the rains pelts. The slightly sloping hallway purifies itself.

Gottfried brings me back to the *Plate* reality. He has written a novel and asks me to review it. The next day I'm sitting in a folding chair in front of the camper and reading his work in the genre science fiction as a beach seller suddenly tears me out of Andromeda. I wince visibly, like an actress too freighted with effects. The handsome boy with blonde dreadlocks is itself quite shocked at my reaction. He apologizes with convincing emotion-filled facial expression that expresses his pity: Sorry, I did not want to... I interrupt him laughing outright; it's okay, don't worry. Had a casting director from Hollywood seen us, we would have been hired on the spot.

Uschi, a woman in her late fifties, visited me for a chat. She is an excellent receiver. Like yesterday, it appears again now, just after I've thought about her she takes place opposite of me. I look at her hands. The saucy Franconian spreads her fingers teasing in front of my nose. Each nail has a different color, blue, yellow, green, pink...

I ask, have you already started with my book? Uschi says, yes, I liked the best with Nena. Where you write, it should be more honest, authentic and less power-hungry people govern. I say: Nena has maybe read the book before you. How so? She is friends with Barbara Simonson that brought me to the Windpferd Publishing. I've sent her two books for Christmas, one for her, one for Nena. I've seen in a TV interview that the pop-Lady had a similar experience. As a child, I also could see my parents as a child as in a soap bubble optically diminished.

Uschi asks, are you going to Morocco again next year? Probably. She says: many campers no longer want to go to Africa. I point with an outstretched arm outside: That does not show. There had been half as many last years. Next year, the fear of the Iraq war may discourage... flirtatiously throwing back her sun-streaked braids, she interrupts me: There are many new ones, but the old ones are tired of Morocco. At the moment, South America and Australia are in full vogue. I nod approvingly, yes, we want to go there also.

The smart Franconian says: We have already booked. The crossing by boat to South America from Hamburg lasts four weeks and costs just for two people with car €3,900 including cabin and meals. I never get Peter thereon, f o u r weeks! Uschi says: But you can go ashore in some ports, anywhere you need no visa. You can forget it. Around the world, I could sail with Peter. But on an ocean liner he feels trapped. He once nearly drowned. We better fly over, buy a RV and meet you half way. Or this way, Uschi throws in forbearing. How long you want to stay, I ask? She shrugs her tanned shoulders, a year or two. Wow! Anyway, you'll hardly be noticed among the locals. With your high cheekbones and the hairstyle, you pass as a Native. Ignoring my Saggy openness the Franconian says, maybe we'll fly home between times. I say: We should first visit Australia. There we have never been. We have friends in Perth and in Surfers Paradise, who visited us once in LA. And Harald Tietze lives near Melbourne. He has visited us recently in Michelstadt. He also writes books. Maybe you know his bestseller about Kombucha. Uschi pulls the eyebrows up and mouth down to indicate that she is not health-conscious. She asks, you know how you have to do it in Australia? I can imagine. Buy the RV in Perth and sell it on the east coast in the best season. Uschi nods approvingly and says: Exactly. I say: By the way, young people can ½ year long work there until the age of 27.

As Uschi has gone, I record the conversation and think about my work. Underway, I scribble my experiences in the waste book. At home, I then brood over the hieroglyphics. In my modern cocoon-like existence, my social life is mainly digital. E-mails are so very easy. Also blogging I could learn now. Under www.marianne-e-meyer.com, I frequently update articles on the net. Less often I'm invited to give lectures or once I was in a TV show. As my tongue often runs ahead from my mind, I feel more comfortable while formulating in written. At bedtime, I'm looking forward to the blissful torture of word coining and the communicating with my readers for their feedback, I heartfelt thank you at this point! Writing can be useful for anybody. While recording our experiences, we can rid ourselves of shame, pain and guilt! Plaguing self-doubt makes just sick. Poetry has a meditative effect. You can be brave, fight hypocrisy and comfort you. Take advantage of the complimentary therapy that makes you laugh or cry! I dream to work like Gauguin on an island in the South Pacific. And I forget in my search for a paradise that I have already found it: here and now at the beach of Taghazout, behind my porch reading or writing under me the pounding surf of the Atlantic. The wave foam slaps are sparkling white against the jagged rocks of the Devil's Rock.

Throughout the morning, Peter tinkers around with the toilet. Since he has acquired an SOG vent and installed, there are no more problems with the toilet. After the air suspension, this was the best getting since the acquisition of the camper. Now we go in good conscience odor- and chemical-free across the country. But this morning I suddenly had the knob in my hand. We had broken a rule:

Never allow anyone unfamiliar to the toilet!

The bumpy access to the sea separates us from Rita and Hans. The latter Bavarian-born Swabian was ten years a service station operator. When people made use of his pump, without having a dime in their pockets, he sucked with a hose the toxic broth out of the tank. So he was catching in the course of time a chronic lymphocytic leukemia. With this autoimmune disease, he lived for 20 years, most cheerfully and happily. His secret: He eats every day three kumquat fruits (fortunella) of his home-grown citrus trees. You can also drink half a glass of beetroot juice or *Green elixirs of life* (Halima Neumann). However, the WBC torment him now and then. When he swings the chemical mace, he is grumpy, and we do better to steer clear of him. 12 years ago, Hans met his funny companion on a journey in a Rotel bus. Rita had recently lost her husband to cancer. During our long beach runs and hiking our affection grows to the chubby Berliner. We discover each time new commonalities. No wonder: she is a Gemini, Libra ascending, I'm a Sagittarius, Gemini ascending and Peter is an Aquarius, Libra ascending. The Ascendant is defined by the position of the zodiac, at the moment of birth. And then the rising star sign influences the character.

I stroll over the sand and gravel covered foothill of the hollow alley to Rita and Hans. Their backpack is full to bursting from the shopping at the nearby Tamrakht. Hans closes the door of the LMC and says, with a relieved sigh, alas, most beautifully it is on the chicken path. Why chicken path? Hans says with a smile: Have you not noticed the women who stagger like drunken chicken down the ravine? I've never seen a drunken chicken. Hans jammed the thumb behind the red suspenders, holding his black leather trousers made in Agadir. He says mischievously, when I was a naughty rascal I have dipped bread in whiskey and fed the chickens with it. They then walked with outstretched wings, so that they could keep the balance. Many of the local women look the same way.

Jokingly I give back, you're still naughty. Speaking of chicken: d'you know the store where the chickens mill around until they are in for it? Rita says: yes, we bought one once. They cost just under 3€ per kilo. They will be weighed alive, then head off and in the plucking machine. This fresh you'll nowhere get a chicken. That's right, if you buy one again, I'll come with you. I cannot choose a livestock and then take it stone dead wrapped in paper home; Peter neither. He said: I'd rather eat only pasta with olive oil.

Back in the camper I imagine this scene with all its horrors again. It is clear to me that I do not even want to be there when others buy a chicken. Although, in the furnished garage-like store the animals are better taken care of than our battery hens. They have at sales times always fresh air and sun. The customers provide diversion when they buy eggs, bread and vegetables. But every entrant could be an extension of their executioner. They witness the killing of their kind, hear the cries, like the cattle and pigs in slaughterhouses, have to witness the massacre associated with low and squeal. Sometimes the animals are skinned still twitching. The Hindus believe in retributive justice: a butcher who tortures the animals unnecessarily will be reborn in the next life in the body of an animal for slaughter. Difficult to substantiate. But: Can you prove otherwise?

Meters high hisses the spray over the rocks. A thought shooting star flashes by ...

With febrile convulsions, I lie in the bosom of my grandma and listen to rising and decongestant sounds reminiscent of blowing a ram's horn. I have visions of earth and fire rollers that break up again and again and continue to rotate...

Peter is with the scooter on the road to get wood to repair the cutlery drawer. Since it is already a replaced part, he has had enough of German workmanship. Jürgen comes to help Peter. Arms crossed over his chest, he says: It is best we do everything ourselves: My F 911 I'd also fit out alone. With a twinkle, the Captain curls his walrus mustache and says mischievously, half a year ago, I set even a chipped tooth with superglue. Has held wonderfully. My dentist advised me to do emergency repairs. You also can do temporary fillings with corresponding adhesive materials. As Globetrotter one can become a generalist. You'll get tips for repairing, healing and sojourn. One of the reasons why migrant birds on wheels live longer than couch potatoes in front of the telly. Once the drawer is fixed, Peter promotes the captain a general.

Hans comes to the door, just as I was producing the modified form of a famous scientist's cancer diet. He asks amazed: What are you doing, why do you need so much linseed oil? I count from 6 tablespoons, mix them with 300 g fresh goat cheese, yellow flax seed and hot spices. I say: This is the oil-protein diet by Johanna Budwig, only you take quark. The lady has already been nominated several times for the Nobel Prize. Hans says, linseed oil I should use only for wood brushing. I said: That would be good for you. Try it, maybe you can tame your leukocytes. It tastes better than you think. Peter eats it even voluntarily. Two tablespoons of it in a deep dish; cut a tomato and half zucchini or cucumber to bits and ready is a first-class meal.

Dr. Budwig has treated cancer patients for 40 years with the oil-protein diet. 90% of

her patients were able to heal themselves.
I offer him the yellow mush on a teaspoon. Here try some. The Swabian retorted: I like nothing now.

On weekends, we have a chance to study from our preferred stand in the first row to the beach the customs of the locals at play. Smoke is hanging in the air. Youths barbecue at the beach. A youngster drums. The other boys and girls clap rhythmically in the hands, chatting and laughing. Nearby, a dozen young men have carved a football field in the wet sand. Two piles of stones on each side mark tiny gates, which are guarded by all players. A Rottweiler puppy runs towards me. His slit-eyed master follows with a surfboard. He asks: Can Lea stay with you? Sure, if she stays. How come you speak German so well? I have lived in Cologne. My girlfriend is still there, but she will soon come, too. I've been 2½ months in Agadir; I already have an apartment. I'm still seeking a location for a restaurant. Well, then we can test your Asian cuisine next year. Since the puppy constantly clears out, I go to the neighbors and make them familiar with Lea. Ultimately, she lies with a German couple's gray poodle peacefully napping under the camper. A Moroccan with a confiding parrot comes over. We talk about politics and history. He's a member of the military and seems to have learned quite another matter at school than me. I have often noticed in discussions with citizens of other nationalities that they had another history approach. Before he leaves, he invites Peter and me to his home for a couscous dinner. I have also noticed that the Moroccans are quite hospitable.

Today, the hawkers hope for better business than during the week. The nut hustler in a blue cotton duster has rehearsed his presentation: The endings of Noix and Cacahouète jolt up with a squeaking "i". Then the gray-curly Berber yells something like Amande, because hazelnuts and peanuts he only hawks almonds. But it sounds more like a cow before milking. Last year, he consecrated in the dunes his boy into the subtleties of the act of nut sale. He practiced with him all pitches.

Social contacts, helpers and social reforms

Like a corpse on holiday sneaks the known all skin and bones Moroccan with leather camels and caught insects in amber. His yellowish parchment skin looks like a drawn skull covering. He holds out some silver chains and bracelets. I ask, laughing, should I get a magnet? Pure silver or not, I do not feel like buying. But I feel sorry for the poor man with his large family. I ask Peter: Didn't we want to get rid of our heavy camping chairs? Good idea. Peter pulls the colorful upholstered parts from the alcove and arranges them in front of the camper. Like the rising sun, the peaked person's sunken cheeks brighten. He is thrilled about the well-preserved chairs. Two he takes at once.

A rail-thin mooch emerges. Under laments, Peter hands him the Marlboro medium carton. He sighs; I will soon myself have no more. Better I buy the local Marquise for Dh15, so the guys do not smoke my preferred brand. Some Moroccans sometimes ask for whiskey or beer. It is not advisable to fulfill the Guardians' wish. They should take care of our cars, not sleep. We pay €1 per night. Only at the Brits at Fisherman's House the Moroccans are still not able to enforce any of the self-proclaimed observation profession. Modern colonialism? Currently, the Islanders are buying on the Iberian Peninsula, meanwhile, they still enjoy the Maggy Thatcher in 1984 enforced reduction British EC contributions. As long as France recoup billions for the chemical farming subsidy from the funds of the EU, the Britons will continue to insist on their discount.

In the hunt of Hash Dwelling's division, the Dutchmen are chief rivals among the European powers. The French keep their distance. Their fathers were rivals of the Britons when they split of Africa. They had built a colonial empire in West and Northwest Africa. Almost all are at Devil's Rock, on The Plate, the campsite or in Agadir. They avoid the vicinity of the Brits. In the surf, a small catamaran is jumping up and down. Already, I'm mentally drifting in the waves of the seventies out to sea.

My companion Peter and Jürgen hang in a stiff breeze in the ropes of a Hobie Cat 16. The two had already taken to the vodka bottle and were a bit tired. The open glider hisses far at full tilt on the spray outside the bay of Puerto Rico, on the Canary Islands. The boys almost touched in a line with the top edge of the water as helmsman Jürgen unintentionally provoked a jibe. Instead of turning downwind, we capsized and splashed in the cold sea. With borrowed friesennerz rain-coat and big boots, I drifted off. Frantically, I tried to capture the oversized footwear by pulling the toes. Concern for the foreign good and the adrenaline rush guided me from thoughts of those sharks off as their obstetrician we had acted in the previous year.

At that time, we were on a commercial fishing boat. The owner caught a pregnant shark female. Most of the babies were driven out by the peristaltic wave. The remaining nine or ten we had to pick and shake until they opened their mouth. The babies were able to survive, but, usually, half eaten by larger fish. 15 of these young sharks might have swum in my vicinity. But my whole concern was loosing the yellow boots. Until we spotted a boat at dusk. The local men came closer. Just as they were giving me a life ring, I thought of the predators. I waited not for the men to pull me on deck, but clawed me on the rope in no time up to the planks. Only when I felt the surface of the ship under me, I was aware of the danger, which I had just escaped. I was trembling, and my teeth were chattering. Two of the fishermen tried to straighten the catamaran, a third poured ½ bottle of red wine down my throat to warm me. Jürgen and Peter did make it alone, but I made up my mind, next time to take a closer look at the people to whom I entrust my life.

On our march from Devil's Rock to Taghazout, we step by Werner and Renate. Years ago, the Straubingers by choice have adopted Tina, a pretty Moroccan shepherd bitch. After the welcome barking, she lies peacefully under the camper. On the adjacent bush sits a jaunty crested lark. Werner raves of the Portuguese Avis (N243):

The campsite in Avis costs nothing. Even electricity and hot showers are free.

I ask: How does that work? The owner is an old Communist. He owns two gas stations, two supermarkets and a restaurant.

It sounds more like a capitalist. Werner says: He believes when people refuel, shop or dine with him they should get something back. They promote his wealth. The camping area is a discount. I say: This confirms the cosmic law, according of which we get rich by giving. At its deepest level, life is a distribution of gifts.

You learn this especially when camping. Here the trade flourishes. It's always about elementary things. Not about glittering Versage rags and designer bags for the price of a used car.

On the way back, we meet another Werner.

At today's wages, an exchange society like the miracle of Wörgl would be useful: A Tyrolean mayor found a solution in the economic crisis in 1932 against the distress of his 400 unemployed community members. He gave out work certificates, which shop owners accepted like normal money. With affixed stamps, the demurrage currency (inventor Silvio Gesell - The Natural Economic Order), was revolving secured. Soon the community coffers were filled with backward taxes. There was a building boom. Until, as before, the authorities intervened in free money experiments in Erfurt and Ulm and the economic miracle came to an abrupt end. (Klaus Rohrbach: Freigeld).

A shock therapy, as experienced by the Kiwis is sometimes a miraculous cure. In the mid80s, New Zealand had its formerly all regulatory officials largely abolished as well as almost all subsidies and forced the citizens back to personal responsibility. The result of this radical cure was low unemployment and illness rates.

The shrink from Friedberg walks his dogs Prince and Leo. We report the free camping space. He said: That is nothing unusual in Portugal. It often happens inland far from the coast. But the social and economic system tailored to the real human nature can not be communism since men want to express their individuality and creativity. They strive to achieve their ideas and gain privileges. Nevertheless:

Everybody has the greatest benefit when it comes to the general thriving which requires equal-opportunity and a functioning economy.

Like in the golden Middle Ages (Karl Walker: Geld in der Geschichte). Then the Brazilian property owners could save their 4 ½ billion dollars for security services annually to protect their home from have-nots. How can we stop that the Happy Few accumulate exorbitant sums, avoid paying taxes and give the governments a chewing out, while the masses suffer? As history demonstrates, it is possible that all people could be doing well.

01-21: Like every Wednesday, we visit Renate and Majid in their house. It sits on the hill behind the police guarded roundabout at the market area of Banana Village. In the summer, Renate leads the Nürburg Lindenhof were the racers, and spectators use to celebrate after a race. Sometimes the boozers end up in one of the rooms of the inn. Peter has met the two through the motor racing and test-driving. Since last year, the house has grown 2½ floors with a view of the Atlantic Ocean.

We look back on the palace grounds of the nearby residing Sheik. Is the Saudi present, stand at the mile-long red wall over a hundred watch-men. High-security measures are the price of immense wealth. *M6* takes it less seriously with his protection. He travels often incognito on the bike. We have observed the king once on jet skis near a yacht off Taghazout. His government people are afraid of surprise visits: According to Radio Camping, he had thrown out a minister, as he had not stayed in office but on the golf course. The press reports: *M6* fired Driss Basri. Under the dictatorship of his father, the hated Interior Secretary was Hassan's henchman.

Renate says: Today we have no water. Whooping with delight, I watch some kids perform awkward jumps in unbridled joy of life. Renate also approaches the kitchen window and rejoices at the young animals of the shepherd who is grazing his herd on the hill. Suddenly she says: Eh! No wonder we have no water. She points down, as it gushes into the ditch. It swells incessantly from the broken pipe. On the beach, a lake forms.

Majid, go call and report the water damage.

Nah! That has long since done somebody. They all have no water. I say: If everybody thinks this way, you will not have water tomorrow. (That's how it was. Majid reported the burst pipe on Thursday. Nobody had taken care of it. Everyone thought Allah will solve the problem.) Renate shows me the garden. The pear tree is tiny. Yes, but it has already born twice two large pears. Hard to believe. But, says Majid, one we even brought back to 87-year-old mother Daun. By the way, after her family, the spa resort of Daun has been named. Really? Yep.

The climate here is like that of LA. We had avocados, oranges, nisperos, and yuccas. The fleshy flowers of the yucca are a delicacy for the Chicanos. They eat them with scrambled eggs. I didn't know that you can eat them. Yes, they even eat cactus leaves. I once read in the L.A. Times:

The cancer rate of Californians is about two-thirds higher than that of Mexicans. Rice and beans are after all healthier as hamburgers and steaks.

Peter urges to leave; we want to get to the market. We park the scooter as usual at the entrance before the first tent. At a slowpoke, who hawks his goods partly on a plastic sheet, partly in the sand, we pick out of a pile of used hardware six rusty herring. After much bargaining and laughter from partially toothless mouths, we pay 15Dh. The patron bagged the money and donated an old scrap of paper. His grandson wraps the nearly foot-long, finger-thick pegs. Now we can fix the satellite dish in the soil. We also want to buy two acid-solar batteries at the metro.

In Morocco, you can get as a tourist with a passport, a day pass for shopping in a metro central market.

01-26: On the road to Agadir, the police stopped us for the first time on all our tours. We were, as everybody else, driving too fast. Usually, only the others get stopped. Ironically, today, we are pushed for time. We have an appointment at 9:30 a. m. at Fiat to order the parts to repair the support bearing. Now it is already 9:37. I pull the vehicle permit from behind the sun visor, submit it through the window and ask: Passport? The policeman says no and looks alarmingly serious. So I reach for my book. The color photo on the cover shows me with Marsha Hunt memorial hairstyle. I laugh and say, je auteur. He does not respond. I say écrivain ... écrire de Maroc. I'm a writer, soy escritor, mi scrittore. A second policeman joins in. He recognizes that the name on the book corresponds with the vehicle registration certificate. Now they smile. One says, aah, écrivaaaiiin, droning in an appreciative coloring. Intuitively, I take up his pleasure about the book that I am writing about Morocco. We are pleased, however, to have escaped a penalty. For Peter, my show was embarrassing. But otherwise we would not have got away without a ticket

**As chaff in the wind -
daily routine on *The Plate***

01-28: We are sitting in the balmy moonlight with a few clouds in front of the camper. Here and there sparkles a star through the dreamlike structures which form the moon and the scurrying clouds. Peter says: I miss the atmosphere around the campfire from last year at the fisher house. I say, then let's just drive over tomorrow. But there are no good places any longer. And we won't have a view like the one there. I look over the blue and white striped porch the street trader persuaded us to buy and ask, what do you think, how many fishing boats are out there? I see 12 lights.

Peter says, oh, we better get father's Sea Eagle. With these antique binoculars, he sees 37 lights, but there are large boats with several lights. Peter says: Some of the campers have guns. I would also prefer to have one. You know what I think of weapons. Peter lowers his sonorous voice emphatically: So far we have never been in a situation where we would have needed one. But now we are in an age where we can no longer fight. From Radio Camping, I've heard that some guys had slashed the tires of colleagues' campers before their eyes. We still have pepper spray, the Mac Light, hammer, knife, my stone collection... with a gun it is easier, impersonal. I do not think I could hit someone with a hammer. If I were in danger, I could do that. At least with a frying pan. Once with Renate Schuster and daughter in our Ibiza apartment, the two slept in a bed before the roof terrace. In the night, Renate woke me up. At the door was a noise. I stayed cool, put on my boots, to defend myself better. With a cast iron pan, I carefully operated the latch and opened the door. Outside it was silent, and we went back to sleep. Peter says, and the velvet voice lowered an octave: My father has once brutally beaten me because I defended myself with a bicycle key. One of the guys wanted to strangle me. The others roared all in agreement. He suffocated me. I just banged him in the face. How old were you then? 6 or 7. Didn't you tell your father that you only have defended yourself? Monosyllabic Peter gasped with a groan; he did not accept it. The boy's father came to our house. You know, we were wine and tobacco wholesale traders. Irritated I say, the business was more important to him than justice, the problem of humanity. Leniently, Peter said: That's how it was in those days. We were only

on Manor Moorbek because of the war. In the country school, five classes have sat in a room. The farmers did not like town children. If you came from the city, you were a prick. And if a farmer came to the royal merchant... he was dependent on the customer. I say, my father had never beaten us. The only time he was close to slapping me when I wanted to help my brother to cut class. I shook the thermometer upside down, so the temperature raised. It fell to the floor and broke. That moment my father came. When his face blushed with anger, I ran out of the house and came back in the eve. Anyhow, he was less concerned with making ends meet. Granny had often cited the Gospel of Matthew from the wrong and the right care, you know, the birds, they neither sow nor reap, but like your father there are many. The father of my girlfriend has even distanced himself from her. I was quite taken aback when at my greeting order to Brigitte's he appalled jerked his eyes open wide and said, I have no daughter with this name. Huh? I first thought to have mixed up persons living in the US for so many years. Later, I tried to understand him. He erased his not adapted to social norms eldest daughter simply from memory to avoid gossip.

01-29: Our neighbors from the new federal states climb the steep chicken path, as Peter comes back from Hans. The Swabian is nutty on the royal war game and had once again managed to convince Peter to a game of chess. I can always make excuses with work. The two Franconian by choice stay for a chat and tell about a Camper-freshman, who had stayed with his new motor home in Casablanca shortly after the bombing. In a demonstration, his car was demolished. Officials told him that he should repair his caravan in Germany. The government would take over the costs. Morocco is not a poor country. My gray cells struggle with the facts of the unemployment rate 20 %, child prostitution, many villages without running water and electricity. No poor country, my ass.

> In May 2003, bomb attacks on Jewish institutions and places of west-secular lifestyle in Casablanca claimed over 40 dead, and some 60 injured. This bombing and two others in August 2003 changed the political atmosphere in Morocco. Politics and society learned for the first time the radical threat of civil society through fractions willing to resort to violence.
>
> A few days after the raids, the biggest demonstration since the independence of Morocco took place in Casablanca. More than one million participants turned against terrorism. After 9-11 in 2001, Morocco has clearly confided to the fight against international terrorism. The security authorities deal with fundamentalist Islamic groups with an iron hand. *M6* has referred to the fight against terrorism and the democratization and modernization of the country as equally important tasks.

Suddenly, the lens opens on El Jadida, a snapshot of our undergo on the first trip to Morocco 1998-99:

We had taken the ferry to Ceuta. On the second day of traveling around noon, we reached the university town. The traffic had come to a slackening. We stuck as well as Ehrhard from New-Ulm and his mother Hanni, who led us in their Clou camper. The Swiss couple who had asked us to take care of their dog and camper in the dreary Spanish enclave were in the middle. The wife's passport had expired. They had to again climb the ferry and take a taxi to Malaga to the embassy. Peter blew the horn. Nothing moved. We did not see what was going on in front of us and only heard horns, whistles, and from farther away wild voices. I asked in the thin air, hey, what's going on? Peter asked annoyed, why does Erhard not continue driving? From a distance, we saw young people in white shirts and blouses come roaring at us. Peter said: What a bummer, just because a fundamentalist Prof has fueled the students, and we have to pay for it. More and more young people crowded the street. Suddenly we were surrounded by slogans roaring students. Peter repeated his mantra, why is he not moving?

> At the time, we did not know what was happening in world politics: After the Iraq again stopped the cooperation with UN inspectors, on the night of 17 December 1998 it came to the first extensive bombing of Baghdad. And we got a reaction from the air raids of the USA and UK.

Brown fists are banging against the windows. Flashes of scorn shoot out of black eyes. Peter moans, just get going. They'll make space. A gripping scene, like in the movies! I bend down for the camera and say, wow that's great pictures. Let it be, who knows how they react. I scream at the young people: what have we done to you? Enraged beautiful grimaces with raven black hair surround us. Neat girls with thick black braids. I think back to photos. Why only nutrition guidebooks? Why not a genre change? Close to shooting against Peters will, I finally refrained from it since doubt prevents me from documenting the turmoil in pictures. Unrestrained the hotheads spit on the windows, louder and louder, the rumble. The door shakes. Lying comfortably on the couch, we let us daily bombard with the manure of horrors. But how different it feels to be among the action! Peter says, now they begin to kick. Hopefully, they jar their ankles. The tires withstand much, but the thin aluminum walls get dents. If we are out of the witch's cauldron, we continue alone.

Some teachers took the young people to their senses. All at once, the Swiss started moving. The Hymer creeps forward, parted the crowd and crushed their shadows under the wheels. But protesters continued to spray their venom and maltreat our vehicle with fists. We could barely look through the window covered with sticky mucus. It looked as if a snails invasion came at us. At the gas station at the end of the village, we washed all the windows and looked at our damages: fortunately not noteworthy. A dent was recognizable only on closer look. On the Swiss motorhome, the plastic of the side window was cracked. On Erhard's Clou, the damage was also limited. All talking across each other we tried to overcome our confusion.

Anne Marie visits to supply us with blue flyers to advertise their laundry shop.

Anne Marie and Ursula operate a laundry shop in No. 51 Khalid Ibn Alwalid Avenue, Agadir, near the post office.

A few days before, she was here with a cameraman and a reporter from the MDR. The TV channel will document how senior citizens from the new federal states make their retirement. To us they came because the neighbors had gathered for a chat, and they had become aware of their speaking in a Saxon dialect. At this early hour of the morning, I was still in my usual posture: with a notebook in bed. Preoccupied with writing, I didn't catch much. Later, Peter said, oh shame you missed it. You should have seen how our neighbor gave the interviewer an ear bashing. His wife interjected that he should stop, but he has always followed the microphone. We have missed you coming up at every turn of the camera from below with your new book, to keep it in front of the lens. Under snorting with laughter, we paint the situation even further:

Gottfried showing up with his Rose of Andromeda. At least as a former GDR citizen, he would have met the criterion. He would not be the first to write his first work in retirement. However, our lives usually provide the better material. I think of Frank McCourt's *Angela's Ashes*.

Strange: Some people behave near a camera like idiots or totally blocked. In *Who wants to Be a Millionaire*, the candidates are sometimes so tense that they do not know very simple things. I can also tell you a thing or two about it. When I appeared as a Spirulina specialist in the ARD Prime channel, I had to guess the most popular song among 4. While the viewers heard all the songs, the last one was Spanish Eyes, I could hear nothing. Excitedly occupied with deciphering the titles I came only up to the third. Of course, I would have chosen the catchy tune, would that have been first on the list. Susanne wanted to enroll me on *Who wants to Be a Millionaire* because I often answer the most difficult questions in her presence. I urged her to refrain from doing so. How embarrassing if I fail at the easy questions. Casually she said, oh, it does not matter. Just hold your book as a mascot in the camera. You know, negative advertising is particularly effective. The people get randy with others making mistakes.

01-30: The support bearing, which we ordered from the ADAC is not there yet. Therefore, we can not make any trips to remote areas. Perhaps we will have to spend our entire stay near Agadir. On the exquisite small promontory, I'm glancing at the Atlantic, at the small communities on the slopes and back over the rugged rocks, spilling out spray. The clouds look like they are from a painter boldly and wildly painted with random brush strokes on the calm blue sky. I think of my successful cloud erasing and concentrate on a small cotton ball and say: The cloud is gone, thank you! All my thoughts and energy I direct towards the volatile ball, I repeat three times: The cloud is gone, thank you. Although there is no motion in the sky, the chosen small water structure has completely dissolved a minute later. Try it sometimes. When you erase clouds, you will be amazed by your power. Whether rainmaker think intensely about black clouds and thank for its existence? To thank and to be strong-willed are crucial.

The rain prayer should be practiced among the Berbers even today. Recently, I read on the internet that in March 2008, Germans made in some villages in the Moroccan Middle Atlas rain with a replica of Wilhelm Reich's Cloudbuster. Every time there was a dark cloud ring which the villagers had never seen like that.

http://claudiabasrawi.wordpress.com/2013/10/10/wilhelm-reich-cloudbusting-in-marokko/

In my book *How Water Connects Our Worlds* (2014/2015) you'll find inventions of Reich, Tesla, Schauberger, and other geniuses who worked for the benefit of mankind on free energy devices. Unfortunately, they have been stopped by greedy bankers, oil and energy magnates who have cheated or killed them.

01-31: Omar, the oil and honey man, comes by on his bicycle. He puts it down and practices a little Arabic with me. Salaam Alai-kum, he says with expecting raised eyebrows. I reply, Alaikum Salaam. He is happy as a child. I ask, do you still carry any argan oil? Without answering, Omar gets 2 liter bottles from the dark brown wooden box that he mounted on the luggage rack of his old bicycle. He had not yet increased its prices. But I should not tell as he gives me always a better price. He may say that to all the campers. The friendly 54-year-old Moroccan shakes my hand and says goodbye, Hamdhullah. I say Alhamdulillah.

But I'm not quite sure whether He exists at all. Who can be sure? When people kill because they do not tolerate that others have a different or no faith, it will be better if there were no religions. Or all three scriptures could be combined. They build very useful to one another: The Torah calls for the observance of the commandments of God; the Gospel calls the charity, and the Koran leads to God. Stefan Effenberger shows in his book *Die Einheit der Schrift* that the discrepancy between the religions is based on misinterpretations. Also, the Yusuf Verse No: 012-111 Khan says: *It (the Qur'an) is not a forged statement but a confirmation of the Allah's existing Books [the Taurat (Torah), the Injeel (Gospel) and other Scriptures of Allah] and a detailed explanation of everything and a guide and a Mercy for the people who believe.*

Islam's prophet, Mohammed, believed Jesus was Allah's anointed messenger. Allah's people (Muslims) are to listen to Allah's messengers (Koran, 4.1715.111)

http://www.islam-101.org/

Would it not be best if everyone treats his neighbor as he wants to be treated by him? Let us better listen to our inner voice, so that the absurdities do not accumulate further. For the so-called God-fighters, it should be crystal clear: murder and suicide are not allowed in Islam. If suicide bombers believe they would go to paradise, they're dead wrong.

At the door emerges a blond bob, under which funny blue eyes beam at me. Rita brings my book back and says: I can not quite believe that we are born again and again. I say, in nature everything is evolving, and nothing is lost. Plug a tulip bulb in the ground: Every spring a larger, more beautiful and more robust flower grows. The tulip bulb branches ever more, larger and stronger. This principle works everywhere in creation. So also the soul develops higher and higher changing bodies. Have you ever looked into the eyes of a child, from which wisdom radiates tow...? Rita interrupts me, but you can not prove it. Yes, I can. The soul is a field. Sheldrake shows thousands of case histories of the seventh sense that telepathy or prediction are innate biological sensory functions. And the physical basis of these senses is the *morphic fields*. Blue eyes look at me quizzically. I say: There are children who speak from their other parents. There's a boy who often spoke of his Mexican mother. He could name the place where he lived with his previous family, claiming to be able to prove it. He had carved into his parents house signs in the window frame. His mother communicated with Professor Hans Bender. The parapsychologist from Freiburg University could find research money and traveled with the child to a small Mexican community. There they found some of the earlier relatives and discovered the engraving in the wood. Rita says: That's hard to believe. But it's proven. There are more cases: So?

In Spiegel TV, a five year-old-boy was once shown, who was in treatment with a child psychologist (Jim Tucker). When he was one and a half year old, he got a slap from his mother Mary. He said, when I was your dad, I never slapped you. Since that time, Maria paid more attention to the utterances of her son. He was born with an underdeveloped pulmonary valve and had heart surgery several times. When he looked at the family album for the first time, he pointed spontaneously on his grandpa and said: That's me! His grandfather had died as a policeman during a robbery in a hail of bullets. The bullet pierced his heart artery exactly at the point where today his grandson has problems. Can you deny this combination of memories and physical hints? Um! There was something else: Once, the boy asked his mother, what was the name of our cat? When his mother called a name, he said, no, I mean the white one. Maria replied, Boston. He cried, yeah right, I always called him boss.

Rita says, well, those are isolated cases, who knows if ... Nooo, I cut her off. I have a friend with similar experiences. And in Spiegel TV an Indian girl was also shown. She was very unhappy because she wanted to visit her other parents who lived near the famous temple. As a child, she had been bumped off a bridge and drowned in the river. Another professor went to the area 600 km away with her. When they came near the temple, the young woman knew of at once and could guide the driver to the house of her former parents. The gripping encounter was shown on television. When the Indian saw her elderly parents, she was like converted and fell on her knees before them. Her behavior was completely changed. The two older people confirmed to have had a daughter who was drowned in the river. Well, ... I could tell you more of Donahue and other U.S. talk shows. There are enough examples. Would parents listen to their children more closely and not dismiss everything as imagination, certainly still a lot of past lives could be documented. I have already experienced so much inexplicable. If you ever walk through a thirty-foot long trench on hot coals without burning the flesh to the bone, then you think anything is possible.

Rita says: I don't know.

Why shouldn't we be born again? The birth itself is already a miracle. Just think of the mystery of the caterpillar turning into a butterfly! Or electricity, the invisible waves that allow you to turning a knob on the radio and listen to any choir, string orchestra or rock song. Hundred years ago, no one would have believed it if it had been described to them.

Hm! Or explain talent, regardless of the parents. How is it that I like to do all transaction on the ground and have no problems walking barefoot through stony riverbeds? Huh? I had twice a dream being a shepherd boy. And how is it that I have learned to speak at the age of ten months already in sentences and read very early? That has something to do with my dream in which I perceived myself in the body of an English-speaking actor.

Would it not make sense if we take skills learned in a previous life, like composing or reading texts, into the next life?

The former life as a mime I've kind of proved in an acting class. During the writer's block seminar with Jocelyn Brando, I got to know two actresses who took me to their acting classes. I decided to learn with Sharon Chatten Strasberg's Method Acting. Huh?

That's a pretty affectionate way to work out roles. In the fourth week, after improvising the play *The Porch*, Sharon spoke highly of me. She said: Great! Great! It didn't look like acting. Before, Sharon had never critiqued anybody this way, not even the stars of our class, like my first improv partner Mariel Hemingway and Christopher Lawford, a nephew of JFK. If I would still work on the associations of my life, it would be perfect. Huh? My partner was not my type. In such a case one has to apply the technique to visualize the object in real love and to be projected onto the partner. The play was about two ex-lovers who met each other after a long time. Anyhow, Sharon said: You have the makings for a great actress. But I didn't want that, all that stage fright, public, fuss. Even before the Improvs I had stomach pain. Why a second time the stress? Learned checked off. I'd rather write in private that now satisfies my need for happiness. And this is what it's all about, to know oneself and the way to be happy. Rita says: There is still much between heaven and earth, which is not explored. The usual peaceful expression returns to her face.

At 18:30, the muezzin calls the faithful to prayer again. I sit sideways on the seat, leaning my head against the wall. With bended knees, I look relaxed out of the kitchen window. Suddenly I see my aura above the knees. Last time I saw this energy field surrounding all living things on a cyclist we met inline skating on a paved forest path in Mümlingtal. I perceived it as a gray contour on his back. My first impression was that this man was suicidal. He might have been in a depressive phase. I hoped that he'll flounder some endorphins. Now, I see the smoky edge around my fingers, and Romy Schneider's paper-thin webbed fingers in the film adaptation of Kafka's *The Trial* comes to mind.

The emissions as a light bulb's escaping electrons show us that we are electrical beings. The more silicon, germanium, selenium and copper we carry with us, the stronger the aura, the further the aura. We can zoom in by our concentrated will. A Texan friend, Lynne Briton, demonstrated this to me at our party.

In my book, Spirulina, *Überlebensnahrung für ein neues Zeitalter*, I show two Kirlian photographs with the energy fields of my fingertips and toes. One was taken before, the other after taking Spirulina. The radiance difference may be because the blue-green algae contains all the semiconductor materials mentioned above in natural, photosynthetically derived form.

Should you ever lack energy, I recommend Spirulina. The filamentous cyanobacterium is referred to in the literature as microalgae. Cyanobacteria have more than three and a half billion years ago started to green the hothouse earth and turned it into a home for aerobes. They produce nitrogen (N_2) amino acids or protein and carbon (CO_2) carbohydrates and release oxygen into the atmosphere. Thus, flora and fauna developed. The blue-green algae contain material and immaterial substances in a balanced form. You could live of Spirulina and water.

If we continue to get our planet dirty and withdraw its resources required for ripening of groundwater, we will sooner or later have to resort to the blue-green micro-organisms.

Currently, in many African countries, projects of self-cultivation of Spirulina are in progress to tackle malnutrition and AIDS. Under the name of Antenna Technologies, Vincent Guidon conducts projects in Mali, Niger and Burkina Faso. Under: antenna.ch you can find out. By the way:

African doctors prescribe their AIDS patients Spirulina, because they realized that the T-helper lymphocytes (CD4 lymphocytes) increased in individuals who had taken it.

Thus, the beneficial microorganism strengthens the immune system. Would the founder of Microsoft, who distributes nearly $3 million for aid programs daily, put emphasis on sustainability, he could a lot accomplish. But this lack the Bill & Melinda Gates Foundation: Neither help cytotoxic drugs for AIDS nor helps genetically manipulated millet against hunger in Africa. The problem with crises is never the seeds, but the soil. If we enrich the soil in a natural way, productivity will follow. GM seeds are only good for Monsanto and the disease business. We do not know what is going on in the cell. Those synthetic genes have a detrimental effect on the immune system. I have shown this in the mentioned book based on studies. The animals that received genetically manipulated fodder had smaller organs than the comparison group; also brains and testicles!

US citizens don't even know what they eat. In 2007, Barak Obama promised that when he'd become President, one of his priorities would be to label genetically modified foods, "because Americans should know what they are eating". But only recently, he deliberated genetically modified foods. Read more:

http://www.jamaicaobserver.com/letters/Barack-Obama-s-empty-promise#ixzz2UEnCbDk5

Rita comes over for a chat. Soon we are in the gap between rich and poor that continues to widen. The ultra-rich could cover the essential needs of the people in the Third World. Their income would still grow, but the population explosion could be curbed. The misery in the poorer countries would finally end. Eh, Rita throws in, where would we be if all people have cars? In my book, I have presented technologies with which we need no fossil fuels. A hundred years ago we could have had free energy from the cosmos, illuminate our homes and drive our cars without dangerous fuels. Our world would not have to be exploited senselessly and ruthlessly. So why is this free energy not used? Because a few greedy people from the stinking energy sectors are not able to get enough. They don't give a damn if everything goes down the drain. They snatch away the patents of the creatives, cheating them out of their genius. Or they stamp them crazy. The Yanks are in this quite large. The US make more on exporting copyrights than on any other product. Due to the exploitation of Mother Earth an enormous gap between rich and poor has emerged. The lack of social opportunities for advancement causes one to be a prisoner of social and economic status, in which one is born. The outward signs of origin have in many countries too much weight. As long as you are recognizable as a member of a low social class, you have no chance of being taken seriously. In USA, I like that you have to look closely to see the most expensive clock on the arm of a man. Even with a Ferrari or Lamborghini in the garage, many drive an old pick-up truck and wear faded jeans, T-shirts and sneakers.

I'm seeking a heart shaped stone for Peter's birthday. When traveling, I write my congratulations on stone hearts or leaves. The dark spot in the distance between the wall of rock and the surf caught my attention: Is it a dolphin? Hopefully plastic! Coming closer, I recognize the corpse of a young dolphin with straight severed tail. Did he fall victim to a propeller? At the Seaworld in San Diego, I once patted such a cute, lively marine mammal. It felt like a tight water-filled plastic animal. I better liked touching the Python on the Venice Beach Boardwalk, warm and soft as silk, so cuddly around the neck.

Elmar visits us with his neighbor Jürgen. The latter strolls about importantly, with a huge camera and stand. Last year we stood with Elmar at the fisherman's house. He had a teacher involved, who taught him Arabic. Some words I copied. But if you speak Arabic, it does not mean that you are understand by Moroccans. There are more Berbers than Arabs. And they have their original languages, which are often only passed on orally.

Elmar's wife is gone. If he treats her like his dog, no wonder she never stays long. The four-legged friend is never out, condemned to permanent homebody. I'm often encouraging and try to offer walking him. But Elmar always reacts with the particularity of the dog. Same with the young greengrocer, I recently asked: Why do I not see any girl on a bike? Hasan pointed to the thighs. He said: No good. I laughed at him and said, you are afraid that they drive off, and you no longer have control. Next time you'll be born as a girl, and

then you will see how it is to be dependent.

How can we have peace in the world, when the sexes are not fully equal? The injustice against one-half of the population favors the adverse living conditions and the bad male habits. You take it from the family to the workplace, to political life, and finally inside international relations. Let's start with the removal of injustice against the female sex in the family! How else can the moral and psychological climate be improved in society, if there is no end to favoring the male offspring in training, recognition of individual achievements, the heir or financial contributions.

Every child should be kept entirely equal within the family. The international peace can only develop when in the nucleus of society justice prevails.

Girls are of little value in Morocco. As Majid's brother was once the best golfer in Morocco, he knows the golf teacher of the prince. From him, Majid knows that the Western-educated princesses are sitting unguarded in the restaurant. In contrast, on the golf course in Mohammedia, everything is safeguarded by security, so nothing harms the king's brother. The third in line to the throne, Prince Moulay Hicha, who is living in the United States, thinks his cousin's reforms are not going far enough. In the mid 90th, he had already publicly called for a parliamentary monarchy. But *M6* does not want to curtail his power. Maybe he'd rather change the constitution and allow a queen to stop the stress. But as long as Islam has no queen, male offspring must be protected. A law in favor of the female sex had M6 but ruled: men can no more repudiate their wives. In the event of a divorce, the acquired assets in a marriage will be divided. *M6* gave his bride Salma Bennani, who carries her reddish colored long hair unveiled, the title of princess. It is a progress. Latefa, the chief wife of his father, one of the 30+ concubines of the harem, *M6* disbanded after his enthronement, was only the mother of the prince.

Jürgen squeezed his six-foot-five into the motor home. Under thinning red hair his features reveal a curiosity, sensuality and cunning. The Northern German says: I heard you write books. How did you find a publisher? The publisher found me. The health expert Halima Neumann visited me in LA. I got one of her books translated into English. She has inspired me to write my thesis on Spirulina. I then learned of a study that

in 1989, Gustafson and colleagues found that the sulfonic parts of glycolipids in Spirulina destroy the "HIV".

At around that time, I voluntarily took part in the AIDS support group founded by Louise Hay. I thought, hey, with the 300 young men who meet every Wednesday in West Hollywood, I could make an empirical study. Once Louise had consigned the group to a colleague, however, only 50 or 60 came.

Jürgen sits there slouching. Water blue eyes staring at me, suggesting, well, what about my question? Yes, the Publisher: The author Barbara Simonson, she also knows Halima, she called and asked if I wanted to translate her book on Papaya. In a conversation, I mentioned my work on Spirulina. Barbara has spoken with the director of the Windpferd publishing house. Monika Jünemann has read a few sample chapters and was hooked. So my career started as a writer.

Flippantly Jürgen replied: So without vitamin B it will not work. I say: If something is to be, it will somehow be arranged. If you can write and have a sense of art, you can also produce a book alone. The water book and this on metaphysics there I've tinkered without help: Layout, cover, everything. But then it depends on marketing. Jürgen purses his full lips and browsing listlessly in *Uebersinnlich in L.A.* I say, looks pretty good, the picture with two faces, huh? He releases a half consenting, half exasperated U-huh. I say: The work of a professional. Ages ago, Lothar Nahler made and sold a whole photo series of me. I'd studied still on the Frankfurt Uni. Jürgen asks what have you written about water? Hm! Water is everything, alpha and omega, the spirit in all things, and a cure-all.

Have you ever heard of the spirit healer Bruno Groening? Jürgen wants to know. Astonished, I yell, you know Bruno Groening? With a jerk, I get up and open the closet door. Under a pile of books, I draw *Wunderwesen Wasser* out and open page 37. Plonking it in front of him, I read: water test with a photo of the faith healer Bruno Groening. Jürgen is unimpressed. How did you end up on the BG of Friends? There are only about 50,000 people worldwide, including 500 university professors, doctors and health professionals. He dodges. I say: For me it was a strange combination of circumstances. Just on the day on which I went for the first time, the water test was on. As if it had been arranged for me. I went as long as was my curiosity satisfied.

02-01: With clear images of a dream, I wake up: I stand on the balcony. Suddenly the ground gives way under me. An ornamental stone sill plunges into the depths. Just when I threaten to drop, I withdraw and simply fly. Out of thin air I conjure a sword and sail as Peter Pan onto a group of wild guys who want to kill an innocent man. The long pointed weapon I stab into an opponent and free the good guys from the clutches of evil. This nocturnal vision reflects my reading: In Philip Roth's American Pastoral, the living underground daughter reported the father of her bombings that killed four people. She lives in a tumble-down neighborhood of Newark. Thieves break in broad daylight pediments out over doorways and cornices decoration of balconies, while the bribed policeman holds his nap.

After a three weeks TV break, we can watch the news again. Following, Miss Marple must defend herself on the deck of a ship violently with an equally long sword as I swung in a dream. Indicates this potpourri of past and future that everything plays in the here and now?

02-02: Hans is standing in front of the camper talking to the neighbors. His parasites have a party, because this morning his stomach protrudes further than usual. Chemoprophylaxis has probably destroyed his intestinal flora. I'm going to advise the Swabian to chase his Candida squadron with colloidal silver.

Colloidal silver acts naturally against bacteria, with no adverse side effects. It does not form resistances. Silver ions have no negative impact on the beneficial bacteria in the gut.

In the supermarket, in front of us a sturdy Moroccan admits his bags in the cart. Two accompanying middle-aged Valkyries stand between us and the wire frame on wheels. Under dresses printed with large flowers, their bodies act as boneless quivering fat. Peter says, do you think he has exchanged them for camels? That must have been quite a herd. Laughing and talking move the merry women their plump bodies forward and help the man packing. The dirty blond Moroccan at the check-out reminds me of Mandira. She also has this lively open nature of our Hindu friend, who lived in the 70s in the same house with us and looked at me as a second mother or a big sister. The young cashier cat-calls at the corpulent Moroccans and then welcomed us slyly smiling in fluent German!

How do you like it here? Puzzled, we respond talking across each other, beautiful, great, we are already the third time with the camper here. The perky woman says, oh, well, you belong to the returner. There are only two statements of tourists: Morocco once and never again and Morocco ever again. How is it that you speak German so well? While the Berber typed our purchases, she says, I am studying German at the University. She does not reveal that she has heard Peters flippant remarks.

While we store our purchases, Jürgen like a phoenix from the ashes stands before the door. Recently, he had driven up with his international specialty bicycle. The windshield is from United States, the rest from Holland and Japan. He took two of my books and has now apparently questions.

Puffing away on a butt, Peter waits outside. Jürgen ducks his head and climbs the steps. He waves a sheet of paper and says: I have to talk to you. I say: We are about to go to the campsite. You can come along. Winking at it, the North German countered: I must speak to you alone. He planted his six-foot-five awkwardly opposite to me on the bench, putting his hand on the table. He complains about the water bottles at his feet. Peter, who has followed the

---

The leading energy practitioner Dr. Robert O. Becker found a correlation between low silver levels and sickness. A person low on silver had more colds, flu, fever, among others suffering.

Cancer researcher Dr. Gary Smith suspects: silver deficiency is one of the main reasons for the existence of cancer. He analyzed hair samples and observed a high correlation between low silver count and disease. See *Tips*, page 84

conversation uninvolved, sticks his head through the door and says: You can cut after. Hoping for a quick chat I give in. I think goodness knows what, but that's probably a macho thing. We go through his list of questions:

Jürgen wants to know if the quality of the water goes down the drain by boiling. No, its cosmic energy and healing power remains. After 5 or better 10 minutes cooking, it is even lighter since the salts deposit as scale. Which device do you recommend for activating the water? I say: I use the GIE activator. (Now the successive model is called Aqua-Lyros and developed by Peter and Isabel Gross. About the circumstances of how it came to changing the company name, I might write a crime novel next year)

With it, even Spain's chlorinated water tastes good. Can we energize water with crystals? Yes, at Berkeley University, it has been demonstrated that plants, minerals and metals left their vibrations in the water. Therefore, the force field of water charged with primal crystal energy acts upon on our body. So it can change the molecular structure of our body water. You can also energize food in water or its immediate vicinity. It, usually, takes 1 to 2 hours. Rock crystal, rose quartz and amethyst should be best. There are even more ways to improve water. If you run it several times through a funnel, it will be right-handed and enriched with more oxygen. Is it too hard, help magnets.

Since I can not catch up with Peter, I ask: What have you done as a social worker? Jürgen says, in the con field and hustler environment. Aha, I think, therefore, the brash nature. Why at age 47 he does not work he does not reveal. However, among the campers we have met next to poor pensioners, who can not afford the heating costs in the Northern European winter, teachers and police officers who suffer of tattered nerves. I say: I would have ended almost in a female prison as well, but opted for an internship in the day care center around the corner. That spun out my energy. At the second field work in a special needs school in a hotspot area, every day I was completely exhausted.

Jürgen had mentioned last time that he knew Schröder from the German SPD youth organisation members. I ask: What's mate Gerhard like? Jürgen says, to a certain degree chummy, but he'd always have things his way. He always wanted to determine. Just like you. Ha ha. Gerhard let no one get hold of himself. Maybe that's the reason he has no own children. As if something had died in him.

We criticize things on others we better work on ourselves. Is he different today than before? Jürgen says: I have no contact. When he strutted around with that thing, you know those long, em ... you mean stilts. That makes him more sympathetic, do you think this was intentional? Jürgen shrugs. I say: Politics is

> Watch your fellow human beings and pay attention to what they have to complain about in others. If you examine people carefully, you will be amazed to find that what bothers them at another, is significantly more distinct on themselves. We are no exception. If we gather all the courage to accept this, we could move a huge step forward in our development. Jesus put it this way: "Why do you look at the speck of sawdust in your brother's eye and pay no attention to the plank in your own eye?"

not for me. I want to be able to say what I think. But instead a badge of honor, I can show a thank you letter from brother John.

From Rau, why? I sent him my books. When he has honored my father for 40 years of membership, I have been sitting at the table with his bodyguards. Somehow I felt, he was not feeling well. He and my father were party pals of the GVP (Entire German People's Party). My old man was a trade representative. He has taken Gustav Heinemann, Johannes Rau and Helene Wessel in his car to campaign events. When it became apparent that the GVP would not reach the 5-percent hurdle, Heinemann advised him and his other passengers to join the SPD. Rau was surprised that my father was only honored now, where it was his turn already a year ago. The pals had thought he was a communist because he had testified for one in court. They refused admission to the SPD until. Later he served the party as leader of the self-employed of South Hesse. Speaking of familial compulsive repetition: The same happened to me at my first students demonstration. I recognized a friend marching behind a red banner, and for a short time walked with him. The state security must have taken photos of me.

Jürgen stares off into space, I know Rau not personally, have made little after the Juso time. The hulk folds the question list. I get up to leave. Suddenly Jürgen pressed out in the timbre of a lament, why after all you two are together? You guys are that different. Whoa! I say shrugging, we know each other from a previous life. His disparaging *Geez!* tells me that he does not consider such things possible. Resenting my *mistake*, for the third time, he rushes to pee outside. When he comes back, I close the door and say with you the Candida albicans has become well entrenched. Exasperated, Jürgen barks: What's that? Saying, read Spirulina, the blue-green wonder, I reopened the door. In this book, I have devoted the invasive yeast ten pages. Those parasites love an acidic environment. They like beer, candy, cheese, bread, pizza, pasta... all the paste fare. Isn't that your favorite food? Jürgen lets out a throaty sound.

When we recently visited him, a huge partially used bar of chocolate lying around with puffed rice, and he drank beer. If you take silver ions or H_2O_2 for a while, and deprive the parasites their favorite delicacy, you're going to get rid of the constant urge to urinate and your tummy. Now I'm going to meet Peter. You can come with me.

While we rush toward Taghazout, I ask: What do you think of the worsening situation by the national debt and the increasingly stringent separation between rich and poor? Do you think we could barter for an authoritarian state again? Oh, I do not know. I say: We need more transparency, responsibility and self-determination. After all, it is our money that politicians are wasting. Going more and more downhill, they'll call again after a f hand. The Nazis may see their chance. Jürgen relents: They will not prevail. That thought the people before 33 too. Our politicians deliver themselves to banks, corporations and other power brokers. They are puppets of the corporate bosses; that indicates the example Stevia.

Jürgen yelps enervated: What's that again? A natural sweetener from sweetleaf, no harmful side effects; banned in Europe (meantime authorized as a food additive since 02-12-2011). Why? We only use problematic sweeteners. Aspartame is a lethal sugar substitute that is found in many convenience foods and cola drinks, also known as Nutra-Sweet, Canderel, Equal, Spoonful or E951. The neurosurgeon Blaylock has found aspartame to cause particularly in conjunction with glutamate or E621 serious chronic neurological disorders. It is responsible for numerous symptoms and diseases: MS, epilepsy, Parkinson's, Alzheimer's, brain tumors, blindness, skin growths, depression, damaged short-term memory or an intelligence weakness.

Geez!

Almost all spice-mixes and instant soups contain MSG or E621. Irresponsible contemporaries burden themselves with bad karma. The problems are known for 30 years.

Jürgen continues his steps with childish vehemence, bowed as if he wants to halt his towering physicality. I'm walking even faster with my 5-foot-five. Why you run so fast? Since I was 19, I keep pace with giants. Edmond was 6.5, Günther 6.6. The same tall was his classmate HP, who centuries ago sent me to Peter for buying a car. By the way, the first one I bought alone and the only one in which I was not duped. Heir of a royal merchant. Why royal merchant? His father was a ship's chandler for the British royal family. Hmm, why are you always come across tall men? As a child, I was teased with my little father that I'd remain a dwarf; likely the reason I passed on the Oedipus complex. Poor Pa!

We reach The Plate. The gentle breeze stirs up dust that dances in the sunlight. I say:

Today, people are manipulated more subtly than in Nazi Germany. It's amazing what they put up with. Many natural remedies that help are not paid from the health plan, because the pharmaceutical industry bribe doctors and politicians and who knows whom else. The sickness industry may also be behind the prohibition of Stevia. Barbara Simonson has written a book about it. The Japanese sweeten more than half of their foods and drinks with this crystalline product, even coke. Why do they force us in this crap stuff aspartame and artificial flavor enhancers, which are responsible for all the recent epidemics ... Jürgen interrupts my monologue: Maybe this is again a kind of Morgenthau Plan, just getting more straight down to the nitty-gritty. Wow, sure! Modern warfare!

Elmar sitting in front of his LMC offers us to take a seat. He tells of a colleague who has a Moroccan woman brought in the camper. He would not do such a thing. Jürgen says: A friend of mine married one. He lives always in stress with this woman and has to feed her family. She works nada. When he asks her to cook or clean up, she throws herself on the floor and kicking like crazy. These women only respond to spanking. He becomes a puppet. I get up, kick a pebble and say, poor final word; I'm going. Attempts to restrain me disregarding, I march towards fisherman's house. From afar I see the General's 911. The two prepare the finest dates and a sun-downer before sunset. Uschi says: Peter has gone. Oh, is it that late already? Then I turn right away. Uschi hands me the noble dish, take one for the way.

The sun has stretched her red band above the clouds. With fast flying legs, I reach he Plate. Crimson sinks our energy giving fixed star behind the torn open cloudy sky. Tangerine fire-like rays gleam above the blue-black Atlantic. Dark protrudes the Devil's Rock from the pounding surf. As I see our Hymer, the fire magic has faded. The sky has turned into a delicate lavender blue violet.

Fetes, sand storms and other challenges

From Sunday to Tuesday or Wednesday the vegetable hawkers withdraw their service. The shops are closed. On Monday Islamism celebrates Aid el Kebir, their most important festival. The feast of mutton reminds of the day when Abraham was about to sacrifice his son to God. When God saw that Abraham was ready, he stopped him, and the child was rescued. In gratitude, Abraham sacrificed an animal. As if God would put a father through so much pressure! Do you think he requires such tests? But Islam demands that believers will show their gratitude when business and health were well in the previous year.

Therefore, every family that can afford it somehow slaughters a sheep. The closer to the feast, the more expensive the poor sacrificial lambs traded. Many children and adult animal lovers feel sorry for the bleating sheep, shackled at the legs. Especially if they are held for weeks in the yard or barn, because six weeks before the festival they cost €150-200. One or two week before you have to fork over €300. After the Fête de mouton, the butchers have holidays as people are tired of the meat. Leftovers go to mosques and to the needy. Last year, Majid's sister from Mohammedia came to visit. She cooked couscous with mutton. We needy ones got the rest. I noticed that the unpleasant sandstorms always rage around this feast. Whether the ghosts do not give a damn about it?

We walk with Rita and Hans to Taghazout. The moist sand is massaging balls and toes. I make sure to leave even footprints and walk like a model crosswise. In the slippery stone passage, I'm meandering about with green lichen covered rocks and take foot baths in puddles filled with stones. As I have overcome the some 70 meters, I turn around. Rita and Hans are reaching the middle. Peter is stalking about with his tender feet in the first third. Thus, an earlier incarnation as a barefoot shepherd boy has advantages.

On the terrace of the *Auberge Taghazout*, Abdellah serves drinks. I enjoy freshly squeezed orange juice at relaxing Rasta sound. We purchased a copy of this very tape on a trip to

Jamaica in the Bob Marley Museum in Kingston from Bob's half-sister Pearl.

The campers who afford the expense of the fence for €3,50 per day, know nothing new. The campsite is almost out of use for us free standing. Earlier we brought letters and cards to the front desk. Today every afternoon a new white Renault van of *La Poste* is driving honking through the rows. We could always stay at our place. In the morning, the boys bring fresh bread. Later, trucks deliver fresh water. Also fruits, vegetables, fish, eggs, biscuits and use goods are brought to our mobile homes. Everything else we can buy in the beach shops and the two villages.

The shoe repairer, tailor and other craftspeople are less expensive than in Europe. Therefore, the campers use to reduce the cost of the tour by taking everything movable in need of fixing along.

On the way back, we pass Hash Dwelling. Norbert, who in the summer lives in a trailer park, immediately opposite the Main University Hospital, is sitting in a folding chair in front of his camper and reading. He has just learned that the property owners want to dissolve the settlement. If he has to leave there, he does not know where he should stay. I urge to go. I'm cold. Minutes pass. I run on ahead. Rita comes with me. An hour later, we crawl up the chicken path up and, because we have no key, sit in front of the camper and wait for the stragglers; I'm shivering. I've not enough flesh on the bones. We stare across the steep scree trail and search the beach for our men. With the beginning nightfall, my teeth chatter louder. For the umpteenth time, I feed the gray gyri of my cerebrum with the bit in the future I only leave the camper with a spare key. Rita says, hopefully, not one of those guys get lost again just as... you-know-who. She alludes to the erotomaniac, who recently pulled out his pecker right in front of her sun lounger. If it had at least been a neat one. The perky Berliner describes the incident again and says: I, of course, went straight into the car. But what could I do now? I say, laugh out loud. I have been practicing this from my earliest childhood on, when nothing comes to mind. I'm always gone well with it.

Laughter is as contagious as yawning and kills fear.

The thoughts shooting star of an upright in a crib sitting baby flashes:

I play sitting in homey darkness. Suddenly, the familiar big girl opens the door and turns on the light. Fear rises! Will she complain? What should I do? For a quick laying back, it is too late. Like hypnotized, I stare at her arm at the light switch and hold my breath as she goes to the closet to get a towel. Turning around, she sees me sitting in the crib. I remain sitting and burst into laughter, my eyes fixed on the beautiful face framed with dark curls. My mother joins in my laughter, not detecting the released weight from my mind. She says, lie down and sleep now. In her voice resonates pride about her spirited in the night not fearful little girl.

So my sunny disposition has been well developed. Later I learned that I wasn't even a year old when I learned the lesson laughter kills fear. When I told this experience to my mother, she was flabbergasted. The disposal of the furniture I had described made it clear to her that this happened at a time when we lived in the Wald St. We moved away from there when I was ten months old!

Peter must not work today, not even ride on his scooter to the market. On birthdays, we spoil each other. I buckle around my back-pack, and trot with Hans and Rita to the fishing sheds over the meadow to the beach. 12 minutes later, we reach the market town in Aourir. I buy one kilo of strawberries, lemons, pepperoni, each a bunch of coriander herb and parsley. The bulk purchase we did yesterday at Marjane supermarket, and there we'd met Mike. In Morocco he is, *wondrously*, always cured of his rheumatic complaints. He had discovered that it's the pork meat. But at home he can not leave the unhealthy smut.

If you can't quit on knuckle of pork and sausage, you better take Spirulina. Because, the alga inhibits inflammation. And therefore it has an analgesic effect.

At home, I make a birthday cake, which consists of only three ingredients. I forgot my electric whisk and have to beat the egg whites with a fork. The almonds I've already ground yesterday. At 12:30, I give the dough into our Italian grill pan with an insert, which we use for casseroles and baking cakes. Hans and Rita appear with their folding chairs. Later, Renate and Majid arrive with lanterns. Majid is tinkering two self-made ones from plastic bottles. I am now fused with the Camper. Only my arms feel the breeze, when I hand a plate of cake, fresh strawberries with cream or more coffee or tea outside. In the camper are 28°C. In the last light of the day, the Atlantic Ocean shimmers pale blue once again before it sinks into darkness. Peter tends the campfire. Hans drags his accordion. While I'm busy with the crushing of garlic and chopping of ratatouille vegetables, a tiny beetle, similar to a June bug, crawls through the strainer. It had probably hidden under one of the tight on the talk of the eggplant adjacent leaves. The vegetables are here, usually, sold as they are harvested. Only on request, leaves and stems are removed. I push my fingers under the Beetle. It climbs it. I bend down in front of the camper and blow it to the ground. The poor guy must get along in a new environment. Allah Ma 'Aki, God be with you.

After the spaghetti Gourmet (see recipes) and plenty of red wine, beer, and for some even hard liquor that our short-term neighbor Jürgen had brought along, we sing and dance through the night. It's still 20 degrees, one of the balmiest nights ever.

02-07: Rita comes with her water bottle on the door. We have an appointment to go to the campsite. The sunshine glimmers surround us. We flick the sandals from our feet and take the first sips from our bottles. I draw with my toes circles in the sand and ask what water are you drinking? You always carry the same Evian bottle. She says: We bought 120 liters of the Spanish water in the 5 liter canisters, which is much cheaper. Of these, I fill this bottle. On the return trip, we fill in pure diesel. I say: Hans can not deny that he is a Swabian. He was probably also inv lved in the invention of the copper wire. Huh? He turned each penny before expending so often until it was a wire. Ha ha! Do you know how the Grand Canyon was created? Nope. A Swabian had lost a dime. Rita likes the picture of the digging Swabian. Suddenly thoughts just come to me, which my tongue hastily transfers, all gushing out of me: We do not come into the world to grow on the material achievements of each life but on the spiritual.

What do you mean?

Our soul experiences a spiritual growth process in the flesh, which is based on the cosmic law. Every action has a reaction in the universe. Every thought, every word and every deed is recorded in a cosmic library, the Akashic records. They are designed to monitor everything. Every time you leave your carnal hull, you can check whether your

life has gone according to plan. If you left one or the other aspect made aside, you can reincarnate in order to make repairs in a new life in favorable time or position of the stars. Your late husband could have come into the world as your granddaughter, to practice, to be less jealous. Rita asks, and for what?

To grow spiritually and be permeated with love. The most powerful cosmic force is love. It stands for living in harmony with all of creation. Every word of love, every good deed that is coming from the heart, set in the world, is forming waves. You can reach the hearts of our fellow men. Every heart that we open through our love becomes the multiplier of that universal love and changes the world.

A few minutes after our return, Rita comes with a short dungarees made of light blue denim and says: Moroccan women may not wear anything like that. It will suit you well. That I do not doubt, I've dreamed of this experience a few months ago. I'd even searched for the shorts afterward when I had forgotten that I got it only in a dream. I go with the pants, a matching shirt and a belt to the bathroom. The latter I need to curb the length. Content, I look at my body in the mirror, the shapely arms and shoulders, a narrow waist, the boyish hips and still firm bottom. With forgiving indulgence, my gaze wanders to the not so tighten thighs. When I went to the gym and kept them fit with a device that reminds of the visit to the gynecologist, they were still tight. I could do something about it. But once the clothes fall over it, the intent is forgotten. It's the same when I look at my no longer fresh face, but with its lively, fickle and energetic expression it still appears youthful. With the isometric exercises already mentioned, I could achieve a remarkable wrinkle management in two applications daily. But the looks in the mirror are rare, and a mitigating veil pull over the partner's eyes. Better wrinkles than fat because wrinkles don't hurt. Obese persons have rarely wrinkles, but often painful joints. The skeleton is not designed for excessive weight masses.

Again the usual on TV: Fear and terror-inducing stuff. What's going on in these young warriors of God, when they meet between hope and helplessness again and again, to plan their attacks? They speak passionately of Allah and the revolution and do not realize that they are going in their unbearable inner turmoil the way that remove them more and more from God. Gandhi and Mandela have achieved with nonviolence more than all the bomb planters and suicide bombers together. They proceed like religious prophets against injustice and oppression. The often unscrupulous acts of the radical holy warriors are only an ineffective counterbalance to their powerlessness and their pent-up anger.

02-11: Willi and Gerti are near Aglou Plage for a few days. We both want to see them again. We also need gas. In Tiznit, the gas is only half as expensive as in Agadir. From Aglou Plage, we call. Gerti will come to the road, so we'll see where we need to go. There are about 16 km in the direction of Sidi Ifni, a city that belonged to Spain until 1969. We pass a waving woman and a wagging dog, who made it not quite up to the road. Peter is always in a hurry, hurry up and wait. In the next village, we call again. Luckily, Gerti has her cellular with her.

Three minutes later, we fall into each others arms. I'll go with the two and let Peter alone cope with the 1½ km extremely rough road.

We enjoy the quiet. Willi is sitting with his fishing rod on the beach. Only his back is visible. After an hour, he trots towards us: Nothing caught. While the men play two games of chess, which Willi loses both, the latter turns on his famous salty Viennese charm. Probably it is not his day. It's good to let the hype of Taghazout behind. I am pleased with the colorful stones that lie near the shipwreck. In my mind, I have already assigned different flowerbeds and bowls. Seashell lovers will also get their money's worth.

02-12: Willi arranges the fishing rod, hoping to finally catch a fish for lunch. Meanwhile, the three of us go on a stone and motif search and discover fantastic mussel beds, a sea full of stones and pink marble formations. I drink up my water bottle and stuff it with small colorful pebbles. We give the area the name Marble Beach. Peter captures a yellow flower, solitary standing in the sand desert digitally. Exhausted, we reach our campers. Willi is all smiles: Gerti disembowels the big fish right away. Our brunch we deserve today. And, fortune seldom comes alone; Willi wins both chess games in the evening.

02-13: A green plastic bucket half full of shells stands in front of the door. I push it listlessly in the shade. Well-meant by the Belgian. He is the only other camper, a hundred yards away, who shares the solitude with us. We are not enthusiastic about this gift because we were fooled in the past week on two specimens that Hans had wanted us to try. Peter suffered for three days. Older people and those with a weak immune system eat better no shellfish, others no more than once a month. Another disadvantage: It uses a lot of fresh water to clean mussels. I bring this bucket to Gerti. She wards off strictly: *Ü wüll se need* (I don't want'em).

We walk along the beach towards Aglou Plage. I snap a shepherd: In the middle of the pink rocks, he washes his animals! Two hours later, we arrive at the camper tired from exploring. With wolfish appetite, I prepare our first solid meal. The Belgian appears, sits down on our camping chair and asks me to come out. While the bread sizzles to freshness, in the Italo-pan with a little water in the lower backup part of the sophisticated appliance, he explains why mussels can be a problem:

You have to scrape the beard and everything hanging out with the knife and wash the mussels several times.

That's very kind of you. I'll tell Hans about it so that he never again poisons his neighbors. Now, excuse me, I've to get to my burning bread. We've not eaten anything today. The Belgian grumbling walks away. I call after him, thanks for the tip. I'm sorry that I've so little time now. The old man goes on bitching. Peter says: That's what you get from your honesty! The people are only happy when they are being lied to. We would've better-thrown 'em into the sea, saying thank you, we'll enjoy'em. That`s the way the son of the royal merchant's speaks. But I'm the daughter of a preacher. I told you from the beginning that you were better off in politics. There you'd have enough opportunity to make people happy with your lies. And we'd be set for life.

02-14: Via rough boulders, it goes back to the road. We are left with the choice to bump over rocks or sink into sand beds. The suspension groans. All over, it creaks and squeaks. In the cupboards, it rattles and shakes. But the support bearing holds. At the campground in Tiznit, we ask for the directions to the gas-works. The colleague tells us:

At the roundabout in front of the campsite, turn left direction Tafraout. After about 1 km turn left. Some 100 meters on the left it is.

02-15: On our hike to the campsite, we meet Manne from Meppen. He is back from his dirt road tour and reports what he noticed while peeing in the middle of the desert: His motorcycle had gone. An iron bolt had broken. He turned around, going back the same way. After 20 km his bike lay there abandoned. He reloaded and affixed it temporarily. Rita and I keep going while the men still talk. Bernhard, a former long-distance runner, comes to meet us. He asks where do you stand? I say, at Devil's Rock, but we will be moving soon after Hash Dwelling. Where is that? At the fisher's house, some call it a Bitch Dwelling. For someone who writes books, the appropriate place to research. Always something going on. Bernhard says: I don't understand that one starts something with local people who are so dirty. His generalization I parry mischievously: We've got showers on board. He ignores my objection: I've never understood why guys go to prostitutes. I do not need that. I say: Maybe they are ashamed because of their individual needs. Or the wicked tempts them. And if a guy is handicapped or ugly as sin, he will never get a lovely woman into bed.

We do not find our men and go back alone. I am once again without a key. Rita provides self-reaped walnuts from their tree on the camping table. I can only eat three or four. Why? They contain lots of the amino acid arginine. I have to watch out to take enough of the opponent-amino acid lysine to prevent an outbreak of cold sores. Lysine you find in most fresh fish, chicken, and goat's cheese.

Whenever I feel an eruption coming, I refrain from hazelnuts and peanuts as these contain three times more arginine than other nuts, almonds and chocolate. Unfortunately in Germany we have no Trader Joe's, where I can buy 100 tablets 500 mg Lysine for less than $3. Huh? Herpes sufferers have to pay ten times as much here. If they nibble one cup of peanuts, they need to take eight tablets to prevent an outbreak. It mounts up!

Out of the magazine rack of the Swabian Berlin Camper collective I fish a GEO with the title: taboo bomb war: crimes against the Germans? Binge-reading, I say: I better never write about it. Why not? The book may be labeled a political book again on Amazon, as *Übersinnlich in L.A*. A kind of modern book burning. Exactly! But when I consider that the Britons in 2002 chose Winston Churchill as the most important Briton of all times before the architect Brunel and Lady Di, the story should be rolled up again. Then rather George Orwell would result on #1 in the BBC poll. It is precisely this transformation of the past as a principle of English Socialism; the visionary has clearly anticipated in his novel 1984. Today his work is even more relevant. Thinking of the bugging affair and implanting microchips! From 2015 on, all babies are to receive a chip as an identity card.

In my childhood Remarque's work, *All Quiet on the Western Front*, was one of my favorite books. It was then lied and lied is today in order to have a pretext for intervention. That also shows the Australian historian Professor Christopher Clark in The Sleepwalkers. He wrote the book on occasion of the 100th anniversary of the outbreak of World War I.

Jung said: One does not become enlightened by imagining figures of light, but by making the darkness conscious. If I'd call the shots, I would urge all countries with a financial incentive to expose their misdeeds to the early history. A global body could take care of any compensation or refund to be paid. If it'd then be accepted that we all are equally good and equally bad, all people would remember every year on a global mourning holiday of all victims. On a bashing day, we could be ashamed for all crimes committed, and on an honor day we would congratulate us that we respect all living creatures and treat them well.

Approach to the past

In the late afternoon, a ragged fisherman comes on the door and asks for bread. Peter says: We do not have much choice, but one with cheese you can have. He cuts the round bread. Its seductive flavor reaches my nostrils. Peter spreads on the butter and a piece of cheese on top, folds it up and presents it to the Moroccan. I drifting in the 1950s and 1960s:

My grandma also shared bread and soup with peddlers. It was a time when the people did not expect anything from the state. Many got trade licenses for traveling salesmen and sold commodities and natural produce. They came with oil, candies, brushes, laces or earthen pots. Grandma sometimes left her purse closed, but then she opened the refrigerator, offering a soup with bread. Before any solid meal, we had a liquid one every day, which makes sense, since we need water for digestion. If we don't drink water or eat soup before eating solid food, our body will obtain the necessary moisture from the cells, therefore it dehydrates.

The itinerant traders fueled our need for entertainment. Later, the dark afternoons followed. We had the first television in the neighborhood. With blinds pulled down, the neighbor kids huddled in a semicircle in front of the boob tube. Then the neighbors came to call since we had the first phone line. Heide Kraft once got my mother out of bed in the middle of the night. Our neighbor's daughter had married a US soldier and forgotten the time difference. But I revenged us with her mother on April 1st. I see the scene before me, as the careworn woman shouted into the black mouthpiece again and again. Until I whooped with delight April Fool. At least I was able to raise her a charming smile.

Without wanting to turn back time, I doubt that our life is more desirable today. Machines steal our work. Especially in Germany everything is highly engineered. Ever more citizens wonder whether politics and economy are dealing in their interest. As traveling people, we see that there are other ways. And we enjoy a few months in our rolling apartment all the interpersonal relationships among campers and locals.

02-20: I sit on the top step of the Hymer and see how the sky above the mountain slopes of Aourir is covering with a looming blackness. Above me, it is still blue. But the scorching sun reminds me of an approaching storm. A furry feeling on my back adds as hardening factor. Rolled there not a thunder in the distance already? Regardless, we want anyhow go to Agadir, to shop and get fresh water. If it gets wet, many campers flee to the metropolis, because they want to be on solid ground in front of hotels or near the boardwalk. On The Plate, you can be stuck for a few days when it rains. Some get so panicked that they fire up their diesel engines at the first hollow tapping of raindrops, and it looks like a procession of dairy vans.

On the road from Agadir to Inezgane, every 20 meters stands a uniformed military guard. It means: The king passes through today. The water at the gas station is running extremely slow. In the meantime, I can wash my hair, and we still have time for brunch. Around 2 p. m. we are on the way to the souk. The troops have withdrawn again. Peter jumps into the market turmoil.

Food and household goods are cheaper in the souk as in the wholesale markets.

I stay in the passenger seat and wait facing a cafe with a huge cola sign. Two men in dark brown robes and knit caps sit right and left from the entrance and gawking. A colorful student crowd ambles past; a beggar fishes yellow plastic bottles out of a dumpster, colorful dressed women ... I would like to take one picture after another out of the open window, but do not have the guts. I'm conflicted between the claim to snag photos for a book and the need not to invade people's privacy. An older man in a blue gown and a white cap comes up to me, reaches out his hand through the window and asks: Ça va? Bien! He says something in French that has to do with taking photos. I point at my books and say: I'm writing a book about Morocco. He asks: Allemande? Oui! He looks even friendlier, gives a condescending nod and a handshake again and walks away. I smile at a withered, sorrowful looking woman in brown djellaba with white flowers. She beams at me. An inner glow brightens her austere features and gives her face a touch of softness back. Faintly, the sun shines through the haze. Four young traffic policemen in red striped gray vests race past on two-wheelers. They stop a white Mercedes cab and control the occupants. The usual hustle and bustle, when the king dwells in Agadir.

Last year the King was in town, we got hit by a truck, directly opposite the cement factory. I asked the doorman to call the police. Is someone injured? No. Then the police won't come. He gave his colleagues notice that he'd go away for a while and went with me to the car. In a touching way he took care of us, sent the guy who caused the accident to the tobacco shop to get an accident report form. He filled out the form for us while Peter informed Renate and Majid by phone. As soon as they arrived from banana village, we drove together to the police to get the protocol confirmed. The official said: This is a matter for the causal agent's insurance.

The accident report we sent to Casablanca and never heard anything from them. We could have spared us the trouble. We have a comprehensive insurance, but, of course, with an accident the premiums always rise.

The fifth needy rummages in the dumpster. Young men with trays of glasses of fragrant mint tea in silver jugs rushing in all directions. Peter takes a long time. Maybe he met someone. In Agadir, we meet more familiar faces than in Frankfurt. After an hour, Peter comes loaded with all kinds of goods on the door. We decide to go to the shop that repaired our accident damage from last year. Peter wants to paint the rims of the Hymer. The workplace manager greeted us with a hello like old friends. Though we only ask for an appointment, his workers want to start right away. The phone rings. My mother says: I was at my tenants. Nushin doesn't mind that you have confused her origin. I say: Oh, good and think she was sent to her from heaven.

After my father's death, the solitary house had been empty for quite a while. All former residents from Eastern Bloc countries and even some homeless were able to build or buy houses. My mother was in despair because she could not find tenants. Eventually, she opened the newspaper and read a want ad of two artists from Darmstadt. She felt that this advertisement had been for her abandoned house. When the couple introduced themselves, she found both very friendly. However, with Nushin's hippie clothes, her extremely long turquoise fingernails and the battered car she doubted their solvency.

Peter knocks on the window, asking if I'd like some tea. The workshop foreman's moon face is all smiles. He celebrates the traditional mince tea preparation. With skillful momentum, he pours the whiskey Moroccan in the glasses and invites all workers and customers. Some revolve around a barrel used as a stand. A man in sea-green hooded coat calls out to me, beautiful mountains. I say, where? Peter says: He just wants to say something in German. I suffuse in the general merriment and treat the men with some dates. Shortly after the rims are painted, it starts to drizzle. We, therefore, remain overnight in the garage. The chef offers us electricity. He lives next door. We see him pottering at his place, lit with a naked light bulb. The moon holds his clouds surrounded belly towards us. I look at it and feel how my blood flows slower through the veins. We should not have rejected the power so modestly because our solar cells could hardly charge at the overcast sky.

02-21: On awakening, a dream of black blood suckers are still on my tail. Two androgenic insects were floating up my scalp to mischief. Half black widow, half tick, the bloodthirsty fellows hid under my hair. Every time I discovered them and shook them off, they were back in a flash even bigger and scarier. What could have triggered this dream?

Perhaps my current reading by Parvin Darabi: Rage Against the Veil. She tells her sister Homa Darabi's story. On 02-21-1994, the Iranian doctor, trained in the USA and peace activist, had doused herself on a populated place in Tehran with gasoline and set on fire. With her action, she protested against the violation of human rights and the fundamentalist laws in their country; to change something. It is inconceivable that a 15-year-old girl is sentenced to be whipped because a strand of her hair peeped out under the veil.

But many parents had been forced to ask Dr. Darabi, her daughters to certify insanity. After all, they would rather accept an ostracism of their children than to lose them to punishment. They were afraid the girls might not survive the whipping. After such an experience, psychological problems are anyhow likely. Maybe my dream was also a response to yesterday's election for the seventh parliament of the Islamic Republic. The conservative bloodsuckers and torturers who want to plunge the country into the middle ages may have triggered it. Only 30% of Iranians have voted. The power of the remaining 70% can, hopefully, prevent the puny scion of the reforms will be trampled. All women have to wear in public the headscarf, the hijab. Would the associated suffering be not so sad, you could burst out with laughter when girls and women are required to wrap themselves in black and cover the hair black. After all, black is the color of power and domination. Only: women must finally recognize and express their power! Resist against the nonsense that men are practicing. Ayaan Hirsi Ali, the Dutch politician, born in Somalia and author of the book *The Caged Virgin*, wrote the script for a short film critical of Islam, which the director Theo van Gogh fell victim. Because of her texts she is highly endangered. She writes e. g., the Prophet Mohammed reminds her of Bin Laden, Khomeini and Saddam. By Western standards, he, who performed the marriage with a nine-year-old (Aisha), was a perverse man, a tyrant. He is a model for all Muslim men and, therefore, it is not surprising that so many are violent. She is accused of throwing the baby out with the bathwater. In contrast, Irshad Manji's book The Departure is praised. It was in the local media hardly noticed as the author speaks to believers as her sort. Instead, Hirsi Ali changed over to the camp of the infidels. Other books on the topic oppressed women in Islam are The Foreign Bride by Kelek or Desert Flower and Desert Children by Waris Dirie, also born in Somalia. A woman cut the top model without anesthesia under blatant hygienic conditions from outer and inner labia and clitoris. Conservatively estimated 150 million girls and women are with a genital mutilation (FGM), of which half a million worldwide live in Europe! About three million girls are mutilated every year. The FGM is a violation that refers to a cultural tradition. In fact, it's about power and control over women. Their sexuality must be destroyed. Whenever these mutilated women give birth, they have to be cut and sewn again. And some dreamers within the scientific world are still surprised by the evenly spread of AIDS across the sexes in Africa! It is quite obvious: next to homosexual behavior, men take drugs and smoke opium or marijuana. Women continue to be violated and used for any dirty work, especially for working within our region of the world long ago banned pesticides. Thus, the immune system is systematically destroyed because it is constantly overworked. Men know women are strong, women also know, but many still suppress and stifle their instinctive wisdom in a quixotic way. Or they expose themselves to paternalism, humiliation, injustice, torture and crimes. We better learn to use our strength for the good of all.

02-22: We have moved to nearby fisherman's house, where we had spent last year most of the time. At Devil's Rock, we stayed so long to please Rita and Hans, though we many a night sat upright in bed and listened spellbound to the thundering spray. The crashing surf seemed to want to drag the camper every moment with it. We now need to assemble, set up and align the manual dish again; an annoying affair that gives us the opportunity to live out our diabolical side.

02-23: Willi and Gerti are back from the south. Somebody had stolen their dish along with LMB. Gerti says: We are to blame. Sindi had barked, but we were too lazy to let her out. I say: Well, Willi may have scoffed at our Oyster that it's given up the ghost. Now he's gotten his comeuppance. It took me long to recognize this principle of cause and effect. Paying attention of our actions and reactions to them, we can avoid a lot of trouble! The little sins are usually punished immediately. The big ones may take many life-times. Gerti says, come over in ten minutes. We'll look after Gabi and Reinhard; they should be back from Dakhla. When I get to the Iveco of the Austrians, Gerti slips me conspiratorially a cigarette lighter. She whispers, Willi must not know that I still smoke. He's quit completely, but I still smoke two or three a day. We find the Clou camper from Rügen. Gabi tells of the grasshopper plague, shows us pictures from the south of the country and gives us fresh, canned green pepper.

Sexology & wishes under the moon atrial

02-24: In Morocco, the earth shakes. Three shocks within 24 hours. After the quake in Macedonia, now France and Morocco are affected. The mud houses are almost all destroyed. The quake in France is above a geological weakness zone along the Rhône and Rhine, in the middle of the European plate. With a 10% probability, Aachen could have an earthquake of a magnitude 7. There, I'd only build like in California: wood or steel frame and plasterboard. Why is the earth shaking as often in recent times? We steal her nutrients! Around 3000 quakes are registered in one year alone, in Lake Baikal in the south of Eastern Siberia. There, the depletion of natural resources is especially rigorous going on, since the area around the deepest lake in the world in extremely rich in metals.

03-03: Like everyday shocks the boob tube with a litany of crimes: 270 people killed in Karbala, the Belgian pedophile Dutroux is at trial. Celebrities also stuck in this morass. Witnesses had been eliminated. Then again the criminal exploitation of the taxpayer: greedy individuals are not able to get enough. It's about excessive subsidies in construction. It makes the poor poorer and the rich richer. Why do we have to bear all the faults of the politicians without directly participating politically? In the United States, citizens can decide on propositions in their states. Germans think of Americans as apolitical because the voter turnout is so low. If we had to make twenty decisions and read forty pages about the pros and cons in order to know what is at stake in every election, the turnout would be equally low. I feel every time taken for a ride when I make my cross and hope someday we may experience true democracy, where the people determine their fate. Why can't we directly participate politically as in USA at federal states level? The caste of politicians may fear, not being able to throw away the taxpayers money anymore. Instead of subsidies and grants, in which the money of the masses is redistributed in favor of a few privileged, there should be tax cuts for all. Would our wages be less taxed, we would not have to rely on government funding and not feel like a supplicant. We could build a house without subsidies. So we'd have what we deserve. Should citizens not get angry when the government makes a mess of their hard-earned billions annually? Is it not a villain, if those responsible cling on their positions or are resigned and payed off worth millions? How long must we console ourselves that no one can escape the cosmic law? Who sows wind makes up the debt by reaping the storm, in this life or the next. The first shall be last; rich misers will be poor and dependent.

Peter asks, do you have any idea why Jürgen is no longer coming? He doesn't know you yet. When I served his coffee with cream, you said, don't spoil the boy too much; otherwise he comes every day. He must have taken it seriously. Peter says, oh, that's too bad; he was quite nice. He made that beautiful poem on your water book. Yes, I say, he is probably a touch me not. But he can dish out himself, permanently correcting people. He reminds me of Bolko, the same voice, and what he says. He even looks like him. Both should analyze their DNA.

03-04: Just as I sit down to feed the laptop with some notes, Ria comes over and says in her funny dutch accent, eh, do you wanna see the pedophile Karl-Heinz, he is just outside. He wears a bright orange jacket and gray trousers. To act inconspicuous, I ask, can I go with Nanka? The doggy is surprised and happy, still a bit hesitant as I get going. Skinny Karl-Heinz is busy with a pile of wood lying next to his Mercedes van. I walk towards the street. Mohammed, from whom I've bought two stones, sits at the roadside with a colleague who deals in imitation Cartier and Guggi watches. He unwraps huge elephants of quartz, tiger eye and malachite. Mohammed says, my family make. Two women on Machin, three men so, he shows with both hands to work with a chisel. I say beautiful, lift the elephant, wow, its heavy. Tiger's eye is for bravery. He does not understand. I say courage. Ah! In California, I walked over fire. Before, each of us got a little stone, tiger eye. We have more courage to walk over the red-hot coals. Mohammed comes back to business, handing me a stone figure. I say, pshaw, much too heavy for the camper. You can bring me small geodes. I indicate gesture to open a hollow stone.

As soon as I'm back on the laptop, Rita and Hans are rushing along from Devil's Rock. Hans has a cold, because it was too cold in the Metro the other day; particularly in the meat department. I pack away the notebook, because the understanding was that I'd march with Rita to the campsite while Hans and Peter play chess. On the way I ask, did you just see a man in gray pants and white shirt? Huh? Ria has last year tried to take a picture when he was in his car just about to sexually abusing a Moroccan boy, who with the lowered pants stood hunched over in front of him. Rita says: Oh that's a disgrace. She wanted to go to the police, but he had closed the door just as she was about to photograph. Yesterday he stood with his Camper diagonally behind us. Two girls came and sat for a while before his mobile. After a while, the pretty one remained, the tall skinny went back to the big camper. There always stay girls. I don't mind. Only when kids have to prostitute... yes, awful! Once, in a street cafe in Agadir two girls with light brown braids approached Peter and me, about seven and nine years old. Nicely dressed with gray skirts and blue sweaters, I wondered why they wanted money or sweets, until I recognized their obscene hand gesture. Shaking my head, they shrugging hopped to the next table.

Jan calls out to us: Piet says, with your Hymer you belong to the plastic camp. Here are mostly converted buses, light commercial vehicles and jeeps. Peter says quite cool: Piet also has an engine. If he doesn't like our company, he can go somewhere else. In the evening, Jan delivers Piet's reply to Peters comment: Of course, with special people we make an exception. We also attract Hans and Rita: It's too boring at Devil's Rock.

While Johannes B. Kerner interviews former Chancellor Helmut Kohl, Peter sits outside all alone by the campfire. Eventually, he comes and says, you have to see that, the moon has a huge halo. Oh, I say, then we can make a wish. In no time, I'm out there, raise my head and catch sight of the greatest halo I've ever seen. They arise as rainbows by refraction. Instead of drops, ice crystals are involved in heights of about 8-10 km. I wish that the whole world reads my books, and they contribute to the regeneration of the earth and to a peaceful coexistence of all residents. Peter says: I hope that I win with your millions, the 24-hour race in a Porsche. I laugh at his profane desire which torpedoes mine in some way.

03-05: For hours a blue compact car parks in front of our RV. Suddenly, I hear Jan call in a resolute tone, if you do that again, I'll call the police. I go out, wondering what's going on. Ria comes in bikini to me and says, the guy in the blue car walked around here looking at me and ... she makes the typical gesture. I say: That happened to Rita on the chicken path also. Last year I was looking at a ledge for beautiful stones. As a Moroccan perched directly above me and spanked his monkey. He was wearing one of these striped nightshirt lookalikes and nothing underneath. At first I thought he rubs his arm until I perceived three arms. The puritanical upbringing of Islam prohibits extramarital sexual intercourse. A man must wait until he has a wife. Only then, sex is allowed. Sexually frustrated, men must stick to masturbation or homosexuality and accidental contacts in crowded, busy places or buses. Also rape is bound to occur with enforced abstinence. Often it remains without consequences for a man.

03-06: Ria dislikes the music that can be heard out of Hans' sound system, Rieu, Strauss & Co. I say: We can tell him to turn the music down. I don't care, but the way we stand, we may hear it less. Hans says: I thought, I'll do you a favor. What kind of music do you like? Ria says: Roy Orbison I could listen to all day. Hans says. Then I had better not played at Peter's birthday. If you do not like it, I could have saved myself the trouble with the squeezebox. In his voice creaks distance. Conciliatory, I say: Oh, that was quite different. That was fun, we all sang, danced and had fun. That was live music. Only every day, I don't have to have it. Hans lamented: Why didn't you say so. Rita sighs: Well, now do not be so offended. That is Hans quickly. Rita thinks it could have to do with leukemia. We know how we are when we don't feel well. The Dutch goes back with me over the stubbly grass. I say: If you fancy Roy Orbison, it may interest you that I know his widow. Ria says: She got burned with her two children. What? When? Barbara in Malibu? I don't know anything about it. Ria says: There is a song, Leah or so, probably his first wife, the children were small. That was in Texas. Yes, yes, I say. Then it can not be Barbara, her sons were already bigger when I met her. My girlfriend has worked for her. When I once visited Ingrid, Barbara had just returned from a wedding in Texas, made us some tea and talked about her flight and the celebration.

The young Moroccan woman who had a rendezvous with the camper walks around with another girl. I smile at her; she beams back in a heart-melting way. Smiling Moroccans look adorable. I can understand, when old geezers like to take in a young attractive girl. At home, they don't get such beauties into bed. We women can be happy that there are prostitutes and we are less bothered. Love is not a sin. It is an absolute life force. Would we love each other, rather than to lie to us, cheat and kill, heaven on earth would be no utopia.

The shaggy sheep bleating graze through. I bring vegetable waste outside. The old shepherdess holds her rags with both hands and hints that she would like to have something to wear. I catch a T-shirt and a pair of socks from one of the storage boxes. Last year I gave her my gray hooded jacket made of silk and a bottle of shampoo. She had quite matted hair. When I saw her again, her hair shone, and she beamed over the furrowed face of wrinkles.

03-07: I sit at the laptop and trying to work. Outside loud palaver. I will not say anything this time, perhaps the lords of creation remember themselves to be less noisy. Peter comes in, gets coffee, says with an apologetic patting of my curls, chatterbox, chatterbox, but sits back in front of the Camper going on babbling. When the deaf neighbor goes away, a trader puts his colorful rugs on our rug and sits opposite Peter. Quietly they talk about the young man's family, the weather in Germany and California. I don't mind at all.

08-03: I'm getting up at 7:30 a. m. Peter also, but only to pee. Coming out of the toilet he mutters: Hardly any water runs; then I'm back to work today. That's what keeps migrant birds on wheels young. In addition to route planning and adjustment to ever new people, there are always minor and major repairs. My eyes are magically drawn to the blinking red bulb above the door. I say: Battery alarm, have you not turned off the receiver?

Aha, says Peter, no need to make anything with the water. No wonder that it is not running. If we don't have electricity. I say if you always turn out first the receiver and then the television this can not happen. Peter replied: The discharge protection should have worked. I've often forgotten things. When the battery is at 11½, the current should have shut down. Perhaps a sign that we should buy the solar batteries? Peter says: Hans has also said yesterday we should buy them here in the Metro. In his catalog they cost twice as much, now God has made the decision for us. Come on Pete, you think He cares about the small stuff? It was rather a good ghost.

One battery Peter hooks up already in the parking lot of the Metro. As usual, he wears his best trousers. It looks now as if a moth flock would have attacked them. The cuffs of the beautiful Norwegian sweater made of cotton has also caught it. I have to knit new ones. After breakfast, we trudge round all streets around the souk to find the public water tap and various accessory shops. From Hans, we have an order to bring some solder. I look up in the dictionary and find solder = souder and tin = étain, so étain pour souder. We find it, shortly after we pass the fish market which is not more than merely an array of rotted wood tables and boxes with corresponding odor. The search for the copper cable is quite difficult. Copper cable reminds me of the self-serving

banker JP Morgan, who torpedoed Nikola Tesla's free energy machine because he had two copper mines. Since copper wires are needed for electric wires free energy would have lessen his profit (see Ferzak: Nikola Tesla and Meyer: Water Connects the Worlds, 2014/2015)

09-03: The handicapped Karl drives on his return from Agadir directly in front of us. He is not to convince that changing 30 meters to the south he'd had a nicer view. Therefore, we move away and have to adjust the satellite dish again. This time worked in no time. We enjoy a much nicer view.

Hans and Rita sit all afternoon in the shade behind their LMC and chat with a fellow sufferer of Hans. The Austrians is also called Hans and another medical miracle. The 60-year-old suffered from inoperable lung cancer at age 39. Only a part was removed. He shows us his scar and says: After surgery, for a few months I have only eaten green stuff, and the knots were gone. But now I can take no more raw food. I reply: There are other diets against cancer. You can go on a strict macrobiotic diet; that's brown rice and boiled vegetables without fat. Or the oil-protein diet by Johanna Budwig. The latter I have tested on my tumor.

In the evening at the campfire, Hans says: In my youth, I drank the milk directly from the farmers, and we were all healthy. I say: It takes many years to destroy the immune system. It makes little sense to drink milk after weaning and then by alien mammals. Japanese traditionally don't drink milk and are in international comparison the healthiest people with the longest life expectancy, despite the two atomic bombs. Hans reacts irrelevantly: The Japanese are all so small and ugly. Instead of commenting his racism and the Japanese regard the bombs as just that, I walk right into the diversion trap by saying: The Japanese consider our long noses ugly as well. Hans keeps quiet. I say:

A disease does not happen overnight. The immune system adapts for many years to unbalanced dietary and unnatural lifestyle. Until there comes a critical incident such as an accident, the death of a spouse or a divorce. In the case of AIDS, the immune system depending on the lifestyle takes sometimes ten years, sometimes a lifetime before giving up. The medics want us to believe the incubation period, the time from infection to onset, is ten or more years. But the name Acquired Immuno Deficiency Syndrome says it clear: It is an acquired immune deficiency. How do you acquire it? By treating the body unnaturally for years. Now after 30 years of AIDS, it is spread by 80% among homosexuals and drug users. If you take legal or illegal drugs every day, your body's defenses become weaker and weaker. Also with anal sex. The skin of the anus is in contrast to the well-padded skin of the vagina fragile and ruptures every time. The immune system must constantly produce white blood cells to repair these wounds. This continuously working immune system weakens the organism over time. You had lung cancer at the age of 39, and it is known, too much animal fat causes most cancers. Your high milk consumption has added up. When the Nazis invaded Holland during the war and claimed all animal products for themselves, the cancer rate dropped in some regions up to 60%.

Sigrid from Minden agrees with me: My daughter was asked by the doctor if she drinks milk. When she said yes, he said, you better stop this in the future, or are you a calf? I say: My mother drinks milk against sleep problems and is constantly phlegmy, choking on mucus. By the way, she will soon be 80 and wants a trip with the Camper. Udo says: You just need a trailer; then she has her separate apartment.

> We thought about a bigger motor home or a caravan. For long-term campers, the latter seems more appropriate. It offers a separate area, a second TV. If the partner is snoring loudly, otherwise annoying or want to watch another program, you can shift to the rear. Disadvantage: Where to park the giant vehicle? We are also not allowed to stand on all places. And how long we can still be in Taghazout on the New Plate is not known.

The interesting topics, whining of the Germans and exploitation of the social system, are broached. I'd like to stay, but go to sleep. The campfire smoke is too much for my lungs.

03-10: Peter lays across from me. His head supports on his elbow. He says: When you were away, Sigrid told us about a guy from Minden, who use to spend many years in the Caribbean. After a few years, he returns to work hard again. I say: It's okay if he earns so much that he can travel again. Peter says, no, his hard work is a different story. He goes to the welfare office to get new appliances, refrigerator, etc., and then sells it all. Really? Yes, and if anyone says this is not a brilliant achievement, if everyone would do so, he insists on his right. The people are quite selfish. I say: No wonder with all the role models that the media shows us constantly. The moral decay is deliberate so that warmongers can make more wars. And who is behind it? Cui bono? Who benefits? Banks and industries. The media, too. At best, we boycott them. The more tricks, fraud and terror, are on the tube, the more crooks and warmongers we breed. It'd be important to motivate people to do something for others. Projects that serve the general public should be presented and awarded as a kind of sport and shown on TV.

Peter changes the subject. He brags about the latest media wisdom: men are at the age of 100 still capable of procreation, women only up to the 50th. I say: Begetting children is easy. If you'd have to bear them, you'd be happy if it were only up to 50. The woman were chosen because they have more endurance than men. Do you know why God created the man first? Huh? He needed a rough draft.

The sun is especially generous today. I go with my notebook to Karl in order to get information on what to do if one wants to carry a young Moroccan woman as a domestic help during the stay. Has the moving been a problem? Not at all! I'm surprised by Karl's physiognomy. Due to the white hair and the mobility problem that imposes him a stick, he looks much older from a distance. But his blue eyes sparkle of a face that persistently resists the ravages of time. Since 40 years, Karl travels to Morocco. Four times he took a girl on his 3-month tours. Sounds like sex tourism? In many cases, this may be true. If a man is accustomed to being cooked and cared for, he wants to take a girl for cooking and cleaning. Karl, who had gone earlier in the week to Agadir to get a pass for his domestic help, says: You have to go to the Honorary Consulate. It has open from 8:00 to 11:00 a. m.. There, you say, I want to invite someone. You get a form, and you fill in the name and passport number of the person you want to invite. Can I request a carer? My mother has a horror of any nursing home.

Mailing addresses: British Honorary Consulate
English Pub, Boulevard du 20 Aout,
Agadir 80000, Morocco
The Consulate General
Diamond House 97/99 Pread Street, Paddington
LONDON W2 1NT

I doubt anyone likes to contemplate on it. In Germany, you have to belong to the top-earners to afford a maid service or a nurse. Karl says: If you want a carer, you go home to the Immigration Office and provide a declaration of commitment that you will pay for the return. This form you send to the invited person. With it, she makes an application for a visa. Then, someone from the Department of Immigration will come to you and check if you live in ordered circumstances and if the premises are given. I say: A room with a roof patio would be free. Fortunately, my mother is still fit.

03-13: Reinhard appears with Blacky. The dog makes himself at home and signals that he unconditionally accepts us as new bowl fillers. His master computer specialist checks to see if he gets the laptop going, but can not do anything. I say: That's the way it is with the computer technology. Input, output, kaput, says the man from Bochum and explains me his theory of relativity: Everything is a relative relation. Sounds tautological, I think. The three dimensions are length, expansion and spin. How do you figure? It has to do with the fact that I only see with one eye. The glasses are so dirty that I wonder how you can see anything at all. In my youth, I'd looked at the world after cataract surgery one-eyed for years. Could that also had consequences in my case?

03-14: The wind today goes to town fiercely, whirling scraps of paper and plastic bags through the air. Therefore, we want to leave a day earlier than planned. As soon as we start to bundle together, the whistling stops, and we enjoy our last day in Taghazout. While we have brunch, the boy with big coal eyes comes on the door. Peter tries to ward him off with a quick No, mercie. That doesn't stop him from stoically unpacking his souvenirs made of stone. Peter sings: Nooo merciiiie. But the 10-year-old places an upright Cobra and two elephants on the floor of the camper, so we can not easily close the door. After Peter's repeated No, he says, manger. Like Al Mundi, who was waiting for his turn, I break a banana from the stalk. With a jubilant melancholic glance, the boy snaps at the banana like a hungry dog after the sausage. He doubts my voice as a woman and fears Peter could say no again. Leaving, he eats his banana with visibly more enjoyment than the cucumber I gave him the first time.

03-15.3: At 11:00 we are still there. Rita comes from the bus. She was at the dentist in Agadir. Serious looking and somewhat breathless she says: Just before my eyes a terrible accident happened. The bus has just held, you know, at the sign from the hotel Imourane. A Moroccan ran across the street to catch the bus to Agadir. He has run in front of a camper's scooter and flung through the air onto the street. It's got them both pretty badly. Turning to Peter, I say: Better only go very slowly at bus stops!

After storing away our belongings, we bouncy move along in the Hymer towards the street. A last look at the oncoming blue-green waves. In a white spray, the Atlantic discharges around Devil's Rock. Currents and smaller rocks act like snorting sea monsters.

The rows of Hymer I, Hymer II and Wrinkly City are thinning. The beach sellers offer their goods now with more persuasion. We spend the last night in front of a hotel in Agadir near the promenade and meet the fun-loving Lilo and her younger life mate. The 83-year-old bundle of energy is interested in my health books. She leads me quickly to the depths of her orderliness. From cardboard food packagings with a stapler, she fixes 5 cm high boxes and puts them lined up flush in the drawers and sorts all the little things clearly and neatly arranged.

Kafkaesque in Marrakech

Once again on the tour I dreamed in the previous night of a baby, but do not remember the content of the nocturnal vision. It supposes to bring good luck to dream of babies. As we pass a casino in Marrakech, I say, maybe I risk a few coins and thinking of Las Vegas.

There I resided with my parents two nights in the Flamingo Hilton and financed our entire stay with only two actions. First I won with the five-dollar chip included in a package deal of $189 five-dollar, betting on 19 without looking. The croupier greeted me every time I walked by, with a joyful smile. With the free coins, I took another $ 25 off a one-armed bandit.

A few years later, we traveled with our US-girlfriend Carole in the motor home to the Mediterranean. In the casino in Monte Carlo, she bought chips and donated me three. I threw one into the machine to pass the time.

There were three blue grapes characters: When I wondered about the missing ringtone, Carole said: You should have thrown all three at once. That was the day after we had been attacked in our sleep.

We stood behind a rock between Nice and Monte Carlo. The next morning, Carole discovered from the alcove window my black leather bag, lonely lying on the road. We missed my credit card and Peters new Calvin Klein Jeans, a present from Carole. In it, he had 140 francs and the car keys. After all, the burglars were kind enough to put the key in the bag. Weak in the knees and feeling like rape victims, we were able to continue. Later it turned out, at 5 a. m., the robbers blue 3,500 francs in a nearby brasserie with

my credit card. Would it have gone differently in the casino when the credit card company would not have taken the damage? A cop in Erbach said, the robbers are obviously in cahoots with the brasserie owner.

Peter ignores my halfhearted proposal to gamble. He is after a carriage ride, probably because we spend the night near the horse-drawn carriages. The first English-speaking driver, I reject. His cab's 121 is digit-sum four! In the most dangerous means of transport, I'm not in for an additional risk. This young man in black leather jacket points to the coach with two gray dappled stallions. They are at the high wrought-iron fence, where overhung blossoms heavy bougainvillea branches whip out of the park. Yes, with the number 151, I am fully satisfied since my birth number is 7.

Peter says: The old coachman with the rusty English is probably his father. We take the places on the rear bank. I ask: Have the horses gotten enough water? Abas responds: These are the villas of rich Moroccan and French. He points to the noble mansions opposite the city wall. I say a shade louder and more impatient, the horses! Cheval! Have they had enough water? L'eau! The old man points to the left gray mold and says this is Mambo, the other is called Jongo. The carriage is number 151. Admitting defeat, I look at the water problem as solved.

Shortly before the Bab Khob runs a boy along and throws me a Bougainvillea blossom on the seat. Abas may think the little rascal is after my digital camera because he is shouting out something to one of the plentiful present policemen and pointing backwards.

Luckily, I always sling the strap around my wrist when shooting the camera. A recommended precaution even without a coach tour, which I'd rather have spared. Maybe it excites me so little because I have gone through the shaking in previous existences sufficiently. A woman in trousers, jacket and scarf, passed us on a moped. In the city, you can see one or another female on a two-wheeler. But in the villages there are not even girls on bicycles.

Mambo and Jongo trot past the walled palm garden where some boys are playing football. While Peter lights a cancer stick of the brand Marquise, I suddenly feel a hand on my neck and scream out. Turning around, I look into the beaming face of a 10-year-old boy, who has probably been a while riding with us. I'm glad that Abas stops half an hour earlier than agreed, not only for the sake of the horses. I cheer, hurray! We're still alive! If I'd not insisted on my lucky number, I'd now probably be without mother's pearl necklace.

On the route to Fez and Beni Mellal, we drive through the lush green level. In the densely populated agricultural area, the people live off olive and lemon trees. The chocolate-colored crests of the small mountain range Jibilet are wrapped in soft blue-green capes. We pass pristine villages on a low-water creek, and on the left an old Ksar. It's surrounded by high walls, the pre-Saharan buildings typically made of mud. The walls are reinforced by corner towers.

Ait Benhaddou, in the province of Ouarzazate, is an enchanting example of South Moroccan architecture. You dive into a medieval world. The mighty gate of the fort was built specifically for Orson Wells' film Sodom and Gomorrah. It towers over several kasbahs. Depending on the angle of the sun, red-brown or terracotta houses of rammed clay extend picturesquely up the slope.

Last year I took my first swapping here. On the souvenir shops the way down to the creek all sellers wanted to talk us into buying something. I said we had no more money. A leather dealer was after my old Nikes. He allowed me to pick anything the store had to offer. Without further ado, I traded the colorful sneakers against a backpack. The nice young man gave me moreover slippers, so I did not have to scramble barefoot up to the camper. He asked me several times if I'm happy with the exchange!

The creek we crossed on sandbags. We were lucky; a film crew was shooting a traditional movie with blue Tuareg, camels and a male music group in white shirts and round caps.

In the studios at Ouarzazate, we saw the scenery of numerous films. We did not even know that they were made in Morocco, such as the film adaptation of Heinrich Harrer's book "Seven Years in Tibet". The young employee of the illusion production facility pointed to the Atlas and said: Here you can see the Moroccan Himalaya. We discovered a large lump of papier-mâché with side panels. The run-down construct was used as an aircraft in the adventure comedy "Romancing the Stone" with Kathleen Turner and Michael Douglas. This film draws me like a magnet and meets the criteria for inclusion in my coincidence collection:

We stayed in a beach community in LA when it aired for the first time in U.S. television. The eventful film begins with writer Joan Wilder, who finished off a novel of adventure after another, without experiencing anything herself, decides with the smashing of a plate to follow her distressed sister in the jungle. I identified with the author and wanted her home along with the cat because I already traveled most continents. I *longed for the peace to writing. Some years later, in a fit of mental derangement, I bought at "A Star Is Worn" on Melrose Avenue, the three-piece whiteA outfit of a blonde top model. In Germany, she was barely known at that time. And I could feel the lines of the white suit Michael Douglas wore in the movie. This thread at the time had cost around ten times more than the corset dresses. Today, the difference would probably be much lower. If anyone would want to buy it at the same price, I payed plus 5% interest: $179.00?*

What's Next? Do I get to know one of the actors of the film personally? Since my father's cousin lives in Jávea in the immediate neighborhood of Michael's property, that would not be so far-fetched.

During the winding drive, I wonder if I could dare to go to the bathroom. I see a sign that asks motorists to buckle up. My imagination runs riot:

I see myself sitting on the toilet seat, Peter yells, cling on tight! A Crash! Splintering wood, cracking and crunching! I fly through the air. We are both fatally wounded. I'll stay for a while, looking at the accident scene and then give Peter a sign that I move out to my mother. I find her sitting in a chair watching television. Because of the electric smog it costs me some effort to make her aware of me. But then I manage just in a fraction of a second to materialize. My mother screams: Nooo! Then tears roll down her cheeks. She sits there as if paralyzed.

The Ferris wheel of a folk festival brings me back to Peter. By the way, my old lady had once such an experience when her mother died at age of 54. She was paralyzed for twenty minutes like glued in a chair at her job. The staff could not help her. A similar experience, I had with the spirit of my mother-in-law on 11-11-1987 in our apartment with the spiritual item 11.

I just came back from the gym in our apartment and looked at the clock. It showed 11:10. So my workout didn't even last half an hour because I became somewhat restless. As I passed on the way to the bathroom in our brand new queen-size bed, I was paralyzed on arms and legs! It felt as if my limbs were filled with lead. I slumped onto the bed. Was I sick? Following a hunch, I asked timidly into the thin air, Lisa, is that you? On the spot, the spook was over, and I could move normally. It had probably been providence that I had just read one of the books by Shirley MacLaine, where I could not have sneaked past. Heaps of the book were sitting on the checkouts of the supermarkets. I told my mother-in-law's ghost that she had left her sick body and is now able to travel at the speed of thought. An hour later, Peter's brother called and confirmed his mother's transition.

Towards my parents, I often mentioned Lisa's bright move with her death date. After all, both sons have difficulties with memorizing data. But who would forget the 11-11? Apparently my mother did not want to stand back and left her body on 1.1.11. Only later, I realized that my father managed to get also the most spiritual number at least as a sum of the digits: 1.10.1998. All coincidences? A likely story!

Water traps at Ouzoud waterfall

We drive through **Tamelelt**, then pass a Ksar with ancient gates. On the right, it goes to Demnate and Azil. To the left, a mountain range extends with bizarre from the bottom protruding rocks. Then large estates, domaines

and rocky mountain ranges with scattered trees on the ridge. After the *Canal Tassaout*, which irrigates the plain between Beni Mellal and Marrakech, the neighborhood appears monotonously. At the junction Azilal, Beni Mellal and Fez, the **Middle Atlas** begins. The following agricultural field crops include olives, potatoes and wheat. While ever again children, adolescents and young adults are waving, we reach the peak of 980 m.

Morocco is a country full of young people. A teenager raises a hand as if he had a cigarette between his index and middle finger. The increasingly dense vegetation is lush and green, with small rock arrangements. In between trees, scattered farmhouses with olive trees, red earth, spurge cushions and then the 500 m deep cut valley of the Oued El Abid. A boy on a donkey beams at us, the sky shows a delicate violet, I would like to paint it. Most campers seem to omit the waterfalls because we have not seen any. In many switchbacks, the road leads uphill through the thuja, juniper, pine and oak forests and offers a unique view of the gorge and the Ait Attab river valley.

Approaching the parking lot in **Ouzoud** in the evening, the way downhill may seem like a dare. The test of courage in the morning I do not pass. A young Moroccan leads us to the river and delivers us to a colleague. This man's mission in life is to lead daring tourists on shaky bare branches above the wild rushing waters. I say, not with me, turn on my heel and elope. After a few minutes, Peter catches up with me. He says I've come to talk with a group of young Moroccans. They asked why I spoke English so well. I've said we have lived long in America. They did not like it. Why? I laughed and said, America is good. They screamed, no, no, Germany good. They stuck their thumbs in the air.

We take the road along the river, looking forward to a flock of ducks and enjoy the tranquility. After a few minutes, a self-proclaimed leader joins us. He just wants to have an American t-shirt. The need for U.S. goods goes hand in hand with the anger about the inequality. He says that the young king was once with a motorcycle at the waterfall. The sun is already high, I hope we are not too late for great pictures. We reach the edge of a small lake, fed by the waterfall. A boatman takes us in a raft, where he merely pulls on a rope that is attached at both ends. An easy way to have free energy. I succeed shooting still some decent photos. A salesman has a beautiful fossil. No way to think about buying anything with Peter in tow. Once back on Ozoud Camping Amalou, we have an opportunity to see a farmer during traditional plowing on the adjacent field. The landscape and the rushing water inspire us. However, the campers' reactions differ greatly: The Austrian Elmar answered my question's about the waterfall with pulling a long face and a bored brow-raising. His compatriot Erika said, wonderful, a must see. We plan next time to stay three days. My intention this time was to shoot some photos for my book on water.

We drive through an enchanting mountain scenery of olive groves, rejoice at meadows with wild flowers, red hills, blue-green, slate gray and red rock formations. A fairytale fir forest, whose fragrant needles form a soft carpet, remind us of the Yosemite Park. Although the trees are not as high as in the United States. On the edge of a pine forest, we celebrate our brunch. A shepherd leads his flock past us. He and his young son assist a goat giving birth. The boy holds the kid up together with the drooping red-purple shiny umbilical cord. At the fisherman's house, just in front of our camper, we've seen the birth of twin kids.

I insert a cassette of Dire Straight, which we so often picked on our long rides through the Wild West because this music emphasizes the solitude of untouched nature mysteriously. Beautiful, all smiling faces, Peter calls out, as we pass three road workers and a young man on a donkey and all wave beaming. We are excited about this unbashful friendliness.

We drive towards the mountain that is over and over dusted with icing sugar as we pass a large riverside laundry. Around twenty young women sit around, relaxed chatting while waiting for their washed and over bushes and trees hanging laundry to get dry. The transport donkeys stand on the sidelines and waiting to be loaded with a fresh cargo. Peter sits visibly amused at the steering wheel, pointing to a further wash happening and a local scrap trade. In **Azil**, we follow the bustle of a large souk with snowy mountains in the background. I would like to shoot some pics. But the feeling, without authorization to enter into a personal sphere, keeps me off. The best is you soon look at everything yourself.

Suddenly we feel like in another country: very clean, many gabled houses, the streets and sidewalks, immaculate. Lakeside, we take a sharp right back past giant cactus bushes. In between sand-colored rocks in red soil. Approximately 300 m after, a double dirt road leads to the tongue of land. Here, an older couple who head a terraced campsite overlooking the lake, welcomes us.

We drive through a military area and are not allowed to photograph. Two soldiers are watching us. The campsite at the dam is abandoned. Therefore, we continue to **Beni Mellal**. The Hymer winds up the pass. There is a warning of ice. Other wheelers are not visible.

By the wayside, children are waving and making different gestures. The older ones wish to smoke. The younger ones tap in turn to the feet, to a T-shirt and to the head. It looks like dancing the Schuhplattler. As still some campers act like a Mardi Gras royal couples throwing candies, the expectations of some children still exist, but hardly in the tourist centers.

Peter discovers another thing Morocco has in common with California: The water flows in pipelines over the mountain. At the entrance of the vitally alive city, an orange blossom scent make us breath deeply. Located on the main street, underwear hanging on a rope stretched between two trees. We look at the **Kasbah Tadla**. A stork occupies its minaret. Shortly thereafter, we see red: Giant poppy fields against the background of chocolate brown Middle Atlas, glowing in the evening sun. In a **Kenifra** residential area near a secondary school, we find a quiet place to sleep.

03-19: On the road again. We enjoy the beautiful mountain scenery. Peter says, as in the Odenwald, only less forest, but higher mountains. Ha ha! The shallow rivulet still trickles through the lush meadows. Rock formations alter the bizarre landscape. Everything is green and blooming. On every little hut sits a satellite dish. A police car flashes past us. Peter says: I feel reassured, even the cops pass on a solid line. Before **Fès**, the tree-lined street is surrounded by a green carpet with orange blossoms. The white royal city leaves quite a desolate impression. On a small elevation framed with an old wall, laundry is hanging on bushes to dry. No construction activities are visible. Peter! Slow down! He fights with the driver of a petit taxi about who is faster on the road narrowing. That sucks! You're a guest here; the man has a job! Men!

Two royal cities and a stormy crossing

We pass a lovely green landscape with red-brown and olive groves. Peter says, like in Salinas. I say, as boring flat, but not as much cultivated as in Northern California. Cheerful free-range chickens and donkeys make this a place where I could reincarnate in a pinch as livestock. As I said, many female Muslims would like to swap with their donkeys.

On the half way to Meknès, again an offset of the Middle Atlas. The construction sand is saffron yellow. Roadside orange sellers offer their juicy goods on rotten wooden carts. 10 km before the royal city, Aladdin's lamp points to a mini-Disneyland. A spherical building is entirely covered with tiny tiles. The region around the nearly 600,000 residents counting provincial capital is very pleasing. The fertile plateau, on which **Meknès** sits 550 m above the sea, is agriculturally intensively utilized. Not until about half way to Sidi Kacem, we pass the famous wine fields of Meknès. Juicy grain fields in various shades of green as far as the eyes could reach. Like a caterpillar a red-yellow train moves on the track, passing huge date palm trees, cacti and olive trees. A beguiling jasmine scent envelops the Elysian scene: a small medieval bridge over a bubbling little creek, in which the sun breaks. Green fleshy leaves bedded in moss grow around rocks of all sizes. Two Berber in blue robes and turbans riding on donkeys in the splendor of the stirred up dust across the bridge and complete the mystical atmospheric picture.

50 km before **Mechra Bel Ksiri** is the area flat again. Eucalyptus trees line the street. We pass several Orange trucks. I breathe in the odor of onion fields. I enjoy watching the beautiful people in pastel-colored Berber wear. On the verge, boys sell vegetables. Goats eat very close to the road, but none of the animals enters the roadway. Even the few-day-old kids know the danger. 75 km before Larache, cows slowly move around since their front legs are tied together, so they can not make big jumps.

70 km before Larache on the right a natural gas refueling station, where we get our bottles filled.

Two boys scuffling; Peter briefly sounds the horn. They wave, then they charge at each other again. Peter has paved the fittings with cassettes and cigarette boxes. I say: How you can see the fuel gauge? Eventually, it makes a hop, and we stay again. 40 km from Larache we finally find a gas station. Many people wear red, wide-brimmed hats. In the middle, they are conical, like the water carriers' hats. We pass a truck fully loaded with sugarcane.

18 km before Larache sits a huge pile of cork oak by the roadside. Hey, that's what Fred wants for his model railway. Peter dreams on. I say, so close we'll never get past these things. Why didn't you stop?

In the next village, Peter buys bread and eggs. All customers are shaking his hand. Since they see little of campers drive through this area, it is a rare pleasure for them to welcome the stranger. A colorful group of women in bright robes is waiting for a bus or carpool. Giggling, some slap their thighs.

Around Larache, farmers sell strawberries most cheaply. We go back to the **Aire de Repos**, free hospitable resting place of the Comarit Shipping Company. It is guarded around the clock. The car-park attendant tells us to go with our passports to the front desk. I ask: Peter, did we have to do that last time, too? The manager takes care of me, while the car-park attendant marshals Peter. The people here are working in two shifts of 12 hours. So it can happen that they are mishearing or misunderstanding something.

Anyhow, we were almost booked on the ship Banasa, to Séte in southern France because the manager Noureddine Salaheddine thought we wanted to change the Algeciras ferry and had forgotten to book. I mention my experience report on our trip. That awakens his zeal. He promptly shows me the facility. For photos, it's too dark. I'll take some pictures tomorrow. The preppy Moroccan speaks fluent German and English. In the summer, he works as a purser on said ship, in the winter here as director. Noureddine proudly presents photographs, showing him with a lace dark blue uniform and his pretty wife in a Berber gown. For the evening, he invites us to soup and mint tea. When we come into the tent, he sits at the table with a lovely couple from France. The two have spent the winter in Zagora. She speaks passable English and is driving a car, he a camper. They commune with walkies-talkies.

I ask Noureddine about the tipping, often a balancing act between praise and insult. Noureddine says: For special services one can give 5 to 20 Dh, but it is not a must. I give the hospitable director my book on water. He hands me the family book, so I note something under today's date. Noureddine's Eau de Cologne accompanies me to the camper, by no means a brand that I would recommend my husband.

03-20: The sun shines for the start of spring as freshly cleaned. I take some photos of facility and staff. In addition to the picnicking area, there is a gas station with car wash and tire service. We can change the front tires with the rear ones for 50 Dh, For additional 6 Dh, we get a thorough car wash including a chassis freed from salt. In between the muezzin calls to prayer. A young believer, whose father lives in Duisburg, is leaving the job for a few minutes to pray. There are neither reservations nor is the work-flow disrupted. It should be every individual's decision, whether and how he or she agrees with the conception of God. I can not imagine Him as such a simpleton that is dependent on being reported on daily formulaic flattery. God is great. There is no god but God. If God is there, He knows himself who He is. I also don't think, He'd care whether we speak to him without shoes or with a tiara. Don't we all pray to the same spiritual energy, whether we call it God, Allah, Manitou, Father or Granny?

Let us reflect daily on the power of love. Let us be attached to this energy! Through love, we are connected with the creation. We better don't act contrary to it by satanic actions, be it by ruining the environment, polluting the air or tormenting and outsmarting our fellow terrestrials. We better recognize that we can create a superior world through the power of our thoughts!

Let us pray for a decent life of all human beings, animals and plants, in abundance and harmony. Let us ask for the strength that we can prove ourselves in His mind. Let us also pray for those who have fled into addiction, so that they get along in the future without drugs, alcohol, smoking or sexual excesses and return to the best possible life.

We drive to the beautiful camping area right by the beach of Asilah. But at the moment, the Andalusian appearing white town just doesn't invite anyone to stop. At this storm, only waves arrive, that resembles milk coffee. The crossing will be rough.

In the port of Tangier, it's as hectic as always. Auxiliary volunteers are fighting for our papers. Do we have successfully repelled one, runs the next to us and calls through the window: Tickets, please. We say no and continue. The next parades the official, pointing to his badge and says resolutely: I need your ticket! I reply: No uniform, no papers. Peter says: We do it ourselves. He takes off. Near the first counter, Peter gets out and presents the entry papers, passports and tickets to the official. I sit in the car and wait. Ten minutes later, he passes, the papers holding up, the other counters. At the last one, a man in uniform takes it from him. I move a few meters. 5 minutes later, Peter shows up and takes over the steering wheel. For a change, we are no longer controlled. A speedboat with little cargo seems to be waiting for us. The height of the ferry is stated as 2.9 m. Peter frowns and says to the employee of the shipping company: Our caravan is 3 m high. He says: Try it. It works without a scratch. The ship is almost empty. Nobody seems to ferry over in this stormy weather.

Sleepless in La Linea

We drive through La Linea and see that the city has changed in the last three months to its advantage: fancy traffic islands, playgrounds, exclusive lanterns. In Spain flourishes the construction sector. It follows the usual procedure in obtaining duty-free cancer sticks in Gibraltar.

03-21-2002: Last night, sleep disturbance was announced. The basses of a disco faded not before 3:00 o'clock in the morning. After brunch, we walk past a blue-washed building with an outdoor terrace in the park opposite. I ask a teenager: ¿Es eso una discoteca? She says: Si. Mental note:

Never spend a Sat night in La Linea again.

03-22: The night before was not much better. A heavy-duty truck run the refrigeration unit every few minutes to keep the cargo fresh. Early on, we walk to Gibraltar to get each a carton cigarettes. After brunch, Peter takes off with his scooter to get his weed of depravity. My proposal to take the camper and duty-free to fill up, he rejected. A little later he comes and says, I had to go to customs. They have entered my passport number.

Shortly after, we walk to the duty-free shopping. The Spanish customs officer says, looking at me: You okay, and with a scowl on Peter, you no. Peter asks: Why not? She says something in Spanish. He replies: You want Gibraltar back and aren't able to speak English. A colleague said: You have to return the bag. I ask: How many times can I get duty-free? Three times within one month, but only once a day. The shopkeeper is familiar with this regulation. He gives Peter a receipt, attaches a piece of paper with his name on the bag and puts it to the other. To the tax collector Peter says: Are you happy now?

03-23: We walk to Gibraltar to release the contraband and even to get one more cardboard of cigarettes. Later, Peter visits the English enclave with the scooter again to look for equipment for a fastening for our satellite dish. Coming back to the same customs officer. He asks him: Have you anything to declare? Peter said: Nope! The official does not look this time and says:

Are you happy now?

To finally have a good night's rest, we go to **Playa Torre Nueva** near Santa Margarita. There, we've a fantastic view of the monkey rocks (see Fig. p.18). After a beach walk, we sleep like a log. A real treat after the uproar nights near the border crossing. Luckily there is no need to get to Gibraltar again since Peter had quit smoking eight years ago.

New acquisition for the coincidence album

We leave the place towards Algeciras/Cadiz and take the exit to Jerez de la Frontera (110).

I wanted to stop here and report on the Iberian Peninsula in the next book. But the small-world story in the Doñana Natural Park, I will not deny you. Therefore, it goes a little further on: The A 381 was once a charming national road. Now it is almost everywhere upgraded to motorway standard, whereby the beauty of the landscape fall by the wayside. Women with richly applied makeup in yellow protective clothing control traffic. Near the second lake, we set off on a road service and have our brunch in the indentation in front of a green iron gate. I just enjoy my 3-minute egg, as a sturdy Spaniard in a dark sporty outfit struggles with his short legs over the wall. He carries a bundle on a stick over his shoulder as Hans in Luck. I say: This is probably a hiker who got a meal. We greet: Hola. He greets back and disappears on the road towards the town famous for its fine sherry. Peter says: Maybe he is a burglar and thinks, these stupid foreigners notice Jack shit! A few brown bulls with thick horns poke along through a lush green mountain slope. In their innocence, they make my heart flutter.

We head towards Seville, past the racetrack, on which the Formula-1 drivers only have their training. Up the hill welcomes us the colorful scrap of a huge construction machinery and tractor cemetery. Shortly before Seville, we take the free highway that goes to Portugal. We make a side trip to the beautiful place of pilgrimage **El Rocio**, where ornithologists take pleasure in a unique birds diversity. Everywhere in this enchanting nature reserve, nest winged warm-blooded animals under the rain gutters. At Pentecost, the believers travel in carriages or on horseback.

In the evening, I cook our usual rice stew. See chapter Recipes. It's quickly ready, and doing the dishes as well. But the rice I rinse very thoroughly. From my boatmen Granny, I know that some ship journeymen pee now and then nonchalantly in the rice heaps.

Prior to the cooked meal, we eat enzyme containing papaya and avocado. Thus, the pancreas has less work. Heat destroys the enzymes. Without these bio-catalysts, we can neither think nor breathe or digest. Do we take none with raw food, the pancreas must produce them in extra shifts. Are we played out, we wonder about our adult-onset diabetes.

Next noon, the rest is the base for rice salad with carrots, endive, zucchini and other raw veggies. The traditional food preparation can be simple. Have a crack at it! Your cells will thank you.

25.3. At the Cuesta Maneli in the **Doñana Natural Park**, we spend the night at the beautiful resting place with a fresh northern breeze. While we make the camper ready, we hear a sound like a balloon. Or is a warship out there? On the path with wooden boards that leads about two kilometers over the dunes to the beach, we stretch our legs. We are surrounded by fragrant mushroom-shaped conifers. As far as the eye can see, only silent trees and the sound of the wind.

I feel like in an enchanted fairy forest in which hundreds of small living temples invite to spiritual composure. Do you know what's the name of those trees? They look like pruned pines. Peter does not respond, as often happens, when he does not know anything. He continues walking while I'm doing two shots and wonder why I know so little trees and shrubs. Forgiving my ignorance, since I'm not all-knowing, I see from afar Peter standing by a younger woman. She seems to be the only one who shares this beautiful world with us. When I arrive, she says after greeting in Frankish colored Bavarian: Do you know that these umbrella pines have come here only in the 18th century? Wow! I say, this fast answer,

I did not expect to my question. How do you know it? I'm a bookseller and editor and explore with my husband the world of trees. The title of the book *Die Welt der Bäume* seems familiar, and indeed the whole scene. The expert says: The umbrella pines can be suffocated by sand drifts. The juniper in contrast adjusts its roots and can, therefore, survive. I say: They probably had more time to adapt. The pines will also manage it.

At breakfast, it dawns on me that the just experienced I had before seen in a dream. Again a déjà vu. I remember that after awakening, I searched for a female author on the internet. But I only found the book *Die Welt der Bäume* by Rudolf Wittmann, recommended for nature lovers. In the dream, I saw a woman and expected a woman's name on the title. Thus, I doubted it was a prophecy. The author, who gains the laurels alone is her husband. It's always the same: The contributions of women are belittled in the male society.

Saddish journey home

On April 7, we arrive in bright sunshine in Marbella. The mood is subdued. In the previous night, Susanne's younger brother Ronny got killed in an accident. In the eve she wants to fly with the kids to Germany. She shows us a recently video made by her brother with himself and the family. It seems that we anticipate our transition into the incorporeal existence. My father collected letters and documents from each year in a folder. On the last one, he wrote: Until end of Sept. 1998. On October 1, he had escaped his physical shell. For Theo Koch, it was similar. Theo and Andrea, the daughter of my cousin Heide, had visited us for the first time together with their children. In the following night, I dreamed Theo got killed in an accident. I informed Peter, my mother and Heide about it. The latter said: That's strange; Theo spoke more often lately about assuming that he would not grow old. Also, he said, I was always very lucky. But now, I have no more guardian angels. A year later, he crashed into a truck and died instantly. Also, before my friend Marita Rohde's fatal accident, a woman in black in a black limousine appeared to her. I also had a prophetic dream about her crashing into a truck just an hour before the twin towers went down. I saw both events months before 9-11.

Since the last new moon, Reinhard's theory of relativity haunts me. Whether a part of my perception may also be different than my contemporaries'? Now and then, in a stage of total relaxation with eyes closed I see three-dimensional scenes from above. In the range of my third eye, I see on a small rectangular screen people of diverse backgrounds running through streets, revolutions, warriors, at the fire dancing natives, light crystals and geometric figures.

In the last night's dream, I was pregnant. My belly felt like a balloon filled with water. A new brain child? Or Reinhard's theory that is always floating around in my gray cells? Has the water belly something to do with the miraculous entity water? Is the water the missing component to duration, expansion and spin?

This fluid is coming from the cosmos as you can see on the NASA picture of this link:

http://www.windows2universe.org/headline_universe/snowball.html&edu=elem

Water is everywhere, in living and dead matter. Even in stones, so they also provide information. The water crystal photos of Masaru Emoto show us: The water is a medium that can be informed by souls. A being that contains more water, therefore, has more intuitive knowledge. Newborns contain around 90% H_2O. Have you ever been looked at by a baby and you felt if it clearly had seen through you?

Masaru Emoto proved with his water crystal photography that the water can transmit vibrations and information of words and thoughts. He informed water samples with positive words or thoughts, such as *Love, Thank you, Mother Teresa*, also with negative, such as *Fool, Dirty, Vicious* or *You make me sick*! The photographed frozen water drops informed positively showed strikingly beautiful crystals. On the negatively informed ones, only fragments of structures were recognizable. Emoto filled water in bottles and pinned labels on it. The effect was like the spoken word. He also filled water with sound; with an edifying, pure music, the structure of the crystal was picture perfect. In contrast, an anapestic beat with short-short-long rhythms produced quite pitiful water crystal images (Meyer 2014/15).

Since we measurably can purify contaminated water through prayers, gentle words or uplifting music, any vibration of our body water will thus affect our being. We have the choice to spoil our body fluids with an anapestic beat. Or we can get it via Bach sonatas or catchy tunes of Elvis or the Beatles in a higher vibration and thus harmonize and balance our body. So praying makes sense before a meal. Singing or thinking positively while cooking or preparing food, will make it better agreeable. Before knowing the water crystal photography, I wondered from time to time: Why do I tolerate an equally prepared dish one time very well, while other times it upsets my stomach? Better we don't cook and eat if anything gets to us or make our blood boil.

Postscript for the not quite convinced reader

My concern is to uncover and disseminate realities, mine and others. If you have read this report about our Morocco travels, you may think I'm slightly exotic, to put it mildly. For, my secondary subjects have to do with past lives, other spheres of perception, synchronicities or prophetic dreams. But the more tangible fields in which I allowed myself to train at three academies could not dissuade me from the cosmic laws. I know from experience that besides the visible world are other worlds, independent of space and time. During writing of *Übersinnlich in LA*, I was aware of:

We live life forward but can only understand it afterward.

We come into the world with likings and talents and use them best in our profession.

Then these individual faculties bring us a rich and happy life. So open the treasure chest of your gifts and bring them into the world! As to the manner born, I've been always motivating my contemporaries. My wish is that we all trust our inner healer, teacher and prophet. This way, our planet will be soon a better place to live. Many things in this book may seem to you incredibly unimaginable, as at first to me. You now have the privilege to take everything, but you don't have to accept anything. Perhaps you have also made one or another affirmative experience. If you want you can tell me about it, preferably by e-mail: DrMarianneEMeyer @ gmail.com or by post: Apto. 320, P-8801 Tavira. Per post, it could take long with the answer because we are often traveling the world. Maybe we'll see you in Morocco or en route. Until then, I wish you on your way into the light all the best, especially always radiant health.

Acknowledgements

Those to whom I owe the most thanks have already gone into the light. My mother Alwine Holschuh and my father Ludwig had always cared lovingly for our cats so we could worry-free travel. Later this had done our neighbor friend Elisabeth Fleischer. Thanks, Csöpi!

Thanks to all Morocco travelers who expressed their experiences with the country and people to me. There were so many that I do not remember all surnames. I thank those that appear in the book and are not mentioned here again. I express my thanks to following persons, for advice, assistance, literature or photos: Uschi & Jürgen Lenz, Rita Staschel, Hans Grombach, Karl Brugger & Loni, Gerti & Willi Wittner, Hedi & Rudi Müller, Susanne Würtz, Gabi & Reinhard Lüth, Rineke Hofman, Helga Evenhuiss, Ingrid Herrmann, Majid Motaib, Renate Daun-Motaib, Elmar Wabnegger, Monika & Gerhard Zinn, Hans Sten and Edith Kohlbach.

Choice of pitches ~ Camper peculiarities

On our previous tours to sunny realms, we found that many in relevant tour guides free pitches have turned into construction sites, hotels, or with low barriers provided parking. Therefore, we advise all newly minted people on the move to keep the eyes open. Often the motor-homes, hidden behind cliffs, piers, coniferous bushes or pine forests, you may detect shining in the sun or moonlight.

In general, the traveling people share information about nice pitches; especially since some campers have no TVs on board and the conversation is a welcome change. So it is advisable for newbies, to keep an ear to the ground when joining a group of globetrotters. From them, you can obtain info on good parking, waste disposal, shopping and waterholes on the route. Every town has a market on a certain weekday. The market days you can find in magazines at newsstands in Spain or Morocco guides. If you are interested in cult sites en route, you can also ask fellow campers. Besides, tourist information bureaus provide proved info based on brochures.

Migrant birds on wheels prefer different pitches, depending on the individual needs. Some are looking for suitable spots where their dogs can run free, others prefer the vital live of the city. Inline skaters, like Erhard, Gerhard and us like to stay on a smooth sub-surface for a while. Latter retiree from Chemnitz we met at the southern end of Puerto Mazzaron. He taught us his latest skills in cross-over, slalom backwards while driving jumping up and continue in the opposite direction. As we skated past a wiry Frenchman with a smooth bald head, he asked Peter in quite passable German: How long did it take you to do it reasonably? Peter said it was quite fast because I ice-skated before. I'll do it for only two weeks. The former handball player said: Although I am already 74, but when you see me next time, I also have such things.

No wonder that campers live longer. You dare to do more of the fun things. Gerhard, who doesn't look retired, was formerly a tennis instructor. He and Rudi, a former manager at Siemens, sometimes prefer wide open spaces with a solid ground, where they can sometimes risk a match. Since I take my racket along, we no longer meet Gerhard. I wanted him to give me a few serving tips.

One of my favorite places was on the coast south of Cartagena, better known as Snake or Hymer Bay. The **Playa de Percheles** in Cañada de Gallego has meanwhile a 2.10 m high bar pushed in front of the coveted leisure colony. However, in the vicinity additional parking spaces are offered.

The **Old Plate** on which many campers were allowed to stand freely because there were hardly any campsites had been vacated in 2005. The **New Plate** is located on the grounds of the former campground in Taghazout. It was closed in 2008 since new campsites, run by owners, were created. Some

Moroccans seem to have reactivated the place. Since the information in the network is contradictory, we want to inform us on the spot. Next year you can learn more about it in my book sequence.

This 2011 uploaded video shows the approach to the new plate:

https://www.youtube.com/watch?v=on18V4TqhMw

Tips

In the **guidebooks & camping guides** for individual tourists traveling through Morocco, you find all major routes and places quickly. The authors frequently revise them (see p.86)

Foods: Except butter and eggs, animal products, such as bacon, sausage and cheese are in Morocco more expensive than in Europe. If you suffer from joint pain, leave them better at home. Chicken and fish are fresh and inexpensive.

If you want to give up **alcoholic beverages**, such as beer, wine and spirits, this is your country. If not, better stock up at home or on the route in France or Spain as they are more expensive in Morocco.

Bottled spring water is also much cheaper in Spain than in Morocco. Some campers buy 5 liter bottles of water in Spain and later fill in discount Moroccan diesel. But of course, more than 20 l is considered smuggling!

Two-stroke oil, petrol and diesel are a lot less expensive in Morocco than in Europe.

Solar batteries are less expensive in Morocco (Metro).

Our **first aid kit** contains plasters and bandages, colloidal silver (liquid micropur) against infections, nausea, insect bites and for disinfection. We can make silver ions ourselves with two rods of 99.99% silver and a 9V battery with clip-connection (red/black cable). Obliged are Japanese mint healing oil, charcoal tablets for diarrhea, and best quality Spirulina. Wound and burn ointment and Cavit dental filling round off the protection. For intestinal problems (diarrhea/constipation) helps psyllium husk powder, for sea sickness ginger; both offers spiraverde.de in best quality. Spirulina intensive care cream with UVA and UVB sun-screens we get at Sanatur. In the bladder and anti-aging problems help cranberries, Astaxanthin, OPC Plus, Green Kamut, vitamin E and other means of survival of drhittich.com

Addresses

Marianne E. Meyer, Apto. 320, P-8801 Tavira drmarianneemeyer @ gmail.com

State Moroccan Tourist Information Bureau
Angle rue Oued Al Makhazine et rue Zalaqa. B. P: 19 Agdal, Rabat. Phone +212 5372-78300
E-Mail: inquiries@onmt.org.ma
http://www.visitmorocco.com/

German Honorary Consulate in Agadir
Consul Honoraire de la République fédérale d'Allemagne, 6, Rue de Madrid, Sect. Résidentiel, 80000 Agadir, Marokko
Tel.: (00212 528) 84 10 25
Fax: (00212 528) 84 09 26
E-Mail: agadir@hk-diplo.de

British Honorary Consulate in Agadir
English Pub, Boulevard du 20 Aout,
Agadir 80000, Morocco
Tel:+212 (0) 537 633 333
Fax:+212 (0) 537 758 709
Email:rabat.consular@fco.gov.uk

The Consulate General
Diamond House 97/99 Pread Street, Paddington LONDON W2 1NT
Tel: 0044 207 724 0624 Fax: 0044 207 706 7407
E-Mail: cg.london@maec.gov.ma

American Embassy in Rabat, Morocco
U.S. Embassy in Rabat, Morocco, 2 Avenue de Mohamed El Fassi, Rabat, Morocco
Phone:212(537)-76-22-65
Fax: 212(537)-76-56-61
http://rabat.usembassy.gov

Emergency calls in Morocco

Police: Phone 19
Ambulance: Phone 15
Accident on highways: Phone 177

Literature

Clammer, Paul, Bainbridge, James et al.: Lonely Planet Morocco. 11th Edition, September 2014

French, Carole: DK Eyewitness Travel Guide: Morocco. Complements *Lonely Planet* quite well. At Amazon you can look inside. 2011

Jakobs, Daniel, Drew, Keith, Hollowell, Thomas: The Rough Guide to Morocco. At Amazon you can look inside. April 2013

Kohlbach, Edith: Mobil reisen: Marokko, 2002. (laufend aktual. CD: www.edith-kohlbach.de) Campingführer Marokko-Mauretanien 2013/14

Meyer, Marianne: Spirulina, Survival Food... Amazing Cures with the blue-green Alga. 20

Roadhouse Aire de Repos in Larache

Favorite Recipes on tour

Eggplant Puree

1-2 eggplant	cut into cubes, in steamer over boiling water cook 30 minutes or fry in pan
2 cloves of garlic	squeezed, add
½ tsp. cumin and some salt & chili	squish everything, allow to cool
5-6 tbs. olive oil and 4 tbs. tahini	stir in
½ cup of yogurt	marinate for a while

Couscous with chickpeas and Harissa

1 cup chickpeas	wash and soak for 12 to 14 hours with
½ tsp. sea salt	covered with water cook gently for 30 minutes
1 cup couscous	pour over 2 cups boiling vegetable broth, let stand for 5 min until the liquid is completely absorbed; stir in
1 piece of butter	leave standing for 10 min, steam for 5 min on low heat
3 green onions	cut into thin rings
10 cherry tomatoes	cut in half
½ bunch of mint and ½ bunch cilantro	chop all ingredients and mix them with couscous

Dressing

½ cup olive oil, 2 tbs. lemon juice and 1 garlic glove	squash and mix with the couscous

2 tbs **harissa** (made of: 3 cloves of garlic, 1 tbs salt, ¼ tbs pepper, ½ tbs red chilli, 1 tbs cumin, ½ bunch coriander; as much olive oil as to get a thick paste; the rest store in the refrigerator.

Chickpea mush (hummus)

2 cups chickpeas	wash, soak and cook as above pestle or blend
3 gloves of garlic	press (garlic press)
3 tbs tahini (sesame paste), 2 tbs lemon juice, 2 tbs sesame or olive oil	and stir in
½ cup yoghurt	garnish with black olives, garnish with

cilantro or parsley, serve with pita bread and salt and pepper to taste

Pumpkin soup with harissa

1 kilo pumpkin	peel, remove seeds & fiber, cut into cubes
330 ml chicken broth	and
1 cup cream	in a pan without lid simmer for 15 min puree, add freshly
grates nutmeg, licorice powder & pepper	add
2 tbs harissa	prep. see bottom left serve with pita bread

Rice with lentils

2 cups brown rice	(optional parboiled) rinse, simmer gently in 4 cups of water
1 cup brown lentils	rinse, cook in 3 cups of water; drain; slice
2 large red onions	thinly; simmer in
5-6 tbs olive oil	for 5 min; add
2 gloves of garlic	press (garlic press) &
some butter and salt	for 25 min; stir in
½ tbs ground cinnamon, ½ tbs paprika (sweet) ½ tbs cumin	and simmer for another few minutes; mix with the drained rice and lentils
1 green onion	and
½ bunch cilantro	wash, chop and stir
pepper and salt	to taste sprinkle with fresh

cilantro (coriander) leaves and serve with rice or pita bread

Fast rice pot

1½ cup parboiled rice cook in 3-4 cups water

1 large onion,
½ red chilicote
1 large aubergine
2 small red pepper — chopped and
2-3 small zuchini — diced
together with and
each ½ tbs cumin &
curcuma (tumeric) — or
Provençal herbs — cook gently; add
2 cups chickpeas — (canned) and stir
1 can tomatoes — season with
vegetable seasoning,
sea or rock salt
¼ cup olive oil — and finally extra virgin

Spaghetti Gourmet

3-4 garlic gloves,
4-6 tomatoes,
1 red peppers,
12 black olives,
5-6 mushrooms
500 g sepia or
calamari pieces
2 cl whiskey,
1 cup cream,
2 tbs herb cheese,
salt and pepper

braise lightly succeeding add and bring to a boil and season with whiskey

Sesame pumpkin cake

100g sesame grinder — grind in coffee
250g hokkaido pumpkin — grate finely
100g butter,
stevia oder xylitol — to taste and
1tbs vanilla or cinnamon — melt in a small pan on low heat, stir, chill
4 yolks of organic eggs
½ tsp stevia or xylitol — to sweeten
2 - 3 tsp Spirulina — im Mixer 3 Minuten lang pürieren, mit
1 dash sea or rock salt and
grated organic lemon — to taste; add the
sesame pumpkin mush — beat
4 egg whites — until stiff und gently fold in

grease a springform pan well with butter, fill in the dough and bake in preheated baking oven at 90° C or 194 ° F.

To preserve all the nutrients and enzymes of the alga, we can use the Spirulina flour for a filling or topping, e. g. make a mousse of 1 cup tiger nut flakes, spirulina powder, xylitol, grates organic lemon and coconut cream. Slice the cake in half and spread the mousse evenly. Or use it as a topping.

Creamy vegetable drink

½ cucumber,
½ red pepper and
1 stalk of celery

clean, chop and liquify

1 cup water
½ Avocado and
1 tbs Spirulina — in a blender; season with
½ tsp sea salt,
½ tsp. chili and
½ tsp ginger

If time is scarce, we can mix Spirulina with an organic seasoning and 3 tbs of rice milk in a cup and fill up with hot water.

This alkaline drink warms the body and cheers up the mind.

The last two recipes are obtained from my book *Spirulina, Survival Food for a New Age.*

Our next tour to Morocco starts from Tavira, Portugal where we meanwhile settled. Unfortunately, the planned one in December 2014 we may cancel. The Federal Foreign Office has warned his citizens to travel to Morocco because of the recent killings by the ISI. Peter doesn't want to lose his head by ultra-fanatical Moroccans. And I am not keen on dying by beheading either. But if we always stand with others I believe we are safe.

The East Algarve Shanty Choir where I am one of the lead singers will not be sad if we stay in Portugal. By the way, we are still looking for good musicians and male singers. We practice at Cafe Kate-Kero in Santa Luzia. **www.eaisc.eu**

Rehearsal at Kate-Kero, Santa Luzia

In planning:
All AROUND WELLNESS CURE WITH PRIVATE RV in a quiet setting near the sea;
Deacidification, Detox, Purging, Weight Loss, Yoga, Breath Walking, Group Therapy
Applications: drmarianneemeyer @ gmail.com or googlemail.com @ halineu

The small seaside town of Manta Rota offers a convenient Motor-home Park at some of the best beaches in Portugal. Nearby another lovely seaside area is Pedras des Rei (right) with its beautiful Barril beach on Ilha de Tavira. There are some places for Motor-homes; one you find just 500 m along the water front on your left.

FOR YOUR NOTES: